CINEPLEX ODEON

The First Ten Years

▪ *A Celebration of Contemporary Canadian Art* ▪
Written by David Burnett

Published by Cineplex Odeon Corporation
Toronto, Canada 1989.

A CELEB

CONTEM

CANADI

RATION *of*

PORARY

AN ART

CANADIAN CATALOGING IN PUBLICATION DATA

Burnett, David.
Cineplex Odeon, The First Ten Years: A Celebration of Contemporary Canadian Art
Includes index.
ISBN 0-9693835-0-9
1. Cineplex Odeon Corporation – Art collections. 2. Art, Modern – 20th century – Canada – Private collections. 3. Art, Canada – Private collections. 4. Artists – Canada. 5. Art patronage – Canada. 6. Motion picture theaters. I. Cineplex Odeon Corporation. II. Title.
N6545.B87   1989   709'.71   C89-093544-0

Published by
Cineplex Odeon Corporation.
Toronto, Canada 1989.
Printed in Canada.

End Papers:
Harold Town, THE FAMOUS
from Universal City Cinemas,

1. BORIS KARLOFF AS THE MONSTER IN FRANKENSTEIN 1931, 1987.
Pencil on NpH rag board.
45.72 x 38.10 centimetres,
(18 x 15 inches).

2. BUCK PRIVATES 1941, BUD ABBOTT & LOU COSTELLO, 1987.
Pencil on NpH rag board.
45.72 x 38.10 centimetres,
(18 x 15 inches).

3. THE PHANTOM OF THE OPERA 1925, LON CHANEY & MARY PHILBIN, 1987.
Pencil on NpH rag board.
45.72 x 38.10 centimetres,
(18 x 15 inches).

CONTENTS

▪ *A Celebration of Contemporary Canadian Art* ▪

4. GARTH H. DRABINSKY,
Chairman, President and C.E.O.
with NATHAN A. TAYLOR,
Chairman Emeritus and Co-founder
of Cineplex Odeon Corporation.

FOREWORD

*This book is both the symbol and
the record of a double celebration.
Nineteen eighty-nine marks Cineplex Odeon's
tenth anniversary – an appropriate time
to look back on what we have accomplished
with pride and look forward to
the future with optimism.*

I have said on many occasions how strongly I feel about the Canadian identity of our Corporation. That feeling grows as our interests and operations spread beyond our national borders. Its expression, however, must go further than mere statements: rhetoric is easy, but must be fleshed out by actions and results. The Cineplex Odeon Art Commission Program, which is the second cause for celebration this book recognizes, is one striking way in which our Corporation has given substance to its identity and asserted that identity internationally.

Our Corporation lives through the widely spread network of its operations. While projects are initiated and decisions are taken at our head office in Toronto, our business is carried out in the hundreds of theatres that feature our name in cities and towns all across North America. It is there, where we come into direct contact with the public, that the strength of our corporate identity must be realized.

Our Art Program is an important contribution in our determination to make our theatres the best possible environment for watching motion pictures.

Through this Program, we seek to enhance the total movie-going experience of our patrons by exposing them to important works of art.

Over the past twenty years many corporations have become major supporters of the arts; the development of corporate art collections has given vital encouragement to the visual arts. I felt that, rather than building an art collection concentrated at our headquarters, the direction we should take was to develop a program that would spread individual works as widely as the operations we run. Such a collection would be appropriate to the character and purpose of Cineplex Odeon. To date, fifty-two of our theatres across North America, from Vancouver to Orlando, and from Los Angeles to Québec City have been included in the Program.

The result is that while many people are likely to see a certain number of the original works, few, if any, can see them all. Hence the decision to publish this book. It enables us, first, to demonstrate what has so far been achieved, second, to introduce the artists to a wider public and third, but not least, to contribute to the general public's knowl-

edge of the depth and quality of Canadian art.

Our Art Program involves many people and I would like to take this opportunity to congratulate those most closely involved with it. The consultant and administrator of the Program is Dr. David Burnett whom I retained in November 1984. He and his wife, Marilyn Burnett, have worked tirelessly since then to build this special collection. They have also been responsible for compiling and producing this book. They both have my grateful thanks. I know that David and Marilyn would want to join me in expressing appreciation to David Mesbur and Peter Kofman and all the architects, designers and project managers at David K. Mesbur Architect Ltd. and Kofman Engineering Services Limited, who have contributed to the success of this Program by designing and constructing the handsome surroundings in which the works are displayed. Thanks are also due to Scott Thornley and Cara-Lynn Rumack of Thornley/Interchange, the designers of this book.

Those entitled to the highest congratulations, however, are the participating artists who have so positively and imagi-

natively responded to the opportunities and challenges presented to them. The results are works of extraordinary diversity and singularly high quality – ranging from minimalist abstraction to painterly figuration, from high realist painting to relief sculpture. And the variety of their work reflects their wide range of opinions on how art should relate to the spaces and context of motion picture theatres. We asked for and received from these artists their creative responses as individuals; collectively, the art they have called into being represents the great range and depth of contemporary Canadian art.

I cannot explain to myself, let alone anyone else, the passion that infuses my interest in the visual arts. I am fortunate to have it; fortunate also that I can translate my belief in the value and importance of art into a form of support that brings it directly to the movie-going public. And, it is a great pleasure for Cineplex Odeon to be able to celebrate ten years of corporate development through the superb achievements of Canadian artists.

Garth H. Drabinsky

INTRODUCTION

A lively and controversial debate in recent years has centred on the issue of art in public spaces. Artists, curators and critics, public and private sponsors, politicians and the public at large are all players.

Actions taken and opinions voiced have brought about close, often surprising alliances among people with widely differing interests, as well as revealing deep disagreements. This is as it should be. Some situations lead to compromise, others remain irreconcilable, but the character of the issue itself prevents there being any broad-reaching resolution.

The very meaning of art, freely expressed, lies as much in the creative reception of art's audiences as it does in the drive of those who produce it. In this, it is a reflection of society and, like society, the condition of art is never static – ideas change, tastes change, styles and fashions mutate and contradict one another. The avant-garde holds no fixed and invariable lead over the art of its time. There is no final image of how art should relate to architecture. There is no immutable distinction between private art and public art. Art is a private activity made public. In the pleasure it gives and the conflicts it raises, it is always a true reference to its time and place.

Corporations, by forming art collections and supporting visual arts projects, have become important participants in the relationship between public art and private art. How they have faced this, and the impact they have had in giving shape to the art of our time, are large and significant matters. This book is the record of how one corporation is making its contribu-

tion to the substance of those issues. Two criteria are fundamental to forming good corporate or private collections. There must be the desire to make a collection, rather than merely to accumulate material, and there must be a determination to seek work of the highest standard.

The Cineplex Odeon Art Commission Program was founded on Garth Drabinsky's belief in the high quality of contemporary Canadian art, and his realization that a meaningful collection for this Corporation would be one that responded to the particular character of its core operation – that of running movie theatres. In precise terms, he wanted to integrate the quality in the art he saw with the image he envisaged for the Corporation's cinemas. The collection thus formed would be uniquely defined.

With Garth Drabinsky's long-held interest in the visual arts, it was, perhaps, inevitable that this should find expression in the image of Cineplex Odeon cinemas early in the Corporation's existence. In 1982, Gerald Gladstone was asked to paint a mural for the Beverly Center Cinemas in Beverly Hills, California. His work, LIFE FORCE, was the first permanent installation of a work of art in a Cineplex Odeon cinema (see p. 11). Two years later Gladstone was asked to produce a second work, this time for the Royal Centre Cinemas in Vancouver. The experience of these moves led Mr. Drabinsky to decide, in the fall of 1984, to

initiate an extensive visual arts program that would be related to the major campaign of cinema building and renovation upon which the Corporation was embarking in Canada. I was retained at this time as consultant to develop and co-ordinate this program that would see professional Canadian artists commissioned to create major works of art for permanent installation in many of the new cinemas being opened across the country. Thirteen commissions were awarded for cinemas that opened in 1985 and 1986 in seven cities.

As the Corporation and its building campaigns expanded, so too did the Art Program. More cinemas in Canada were included, and in May 1987 the first work of art was installed in a cinema in the United States. To date, works of art in fifty-two cinemas comprise the Art Program, thirty-one in Canada and twenty-one in the United States spreading across five provinces, ten states and the District of Columbia.

In view of the range of art that could be anticipated, and the variety of spaces in which the works would be installed, the guidelines and procedures of the Art Program had to balance flexibility with consistent expectations. It was decided at the outset that commissions for cinemas in Canada would be awarded on a regional basis – an artist would be chosen from among those who came from, or worked in, the area where a particular cinema was located. In this way the Art Program,

5. FANTASY CINEMAS. *New York (Rockville Centre), New York.*

like other aspects of the Corporation's operations, would underline the commitment of the Corporation to the communities it serves. Further, it was important that the support given to artists should assist them in being recognized in their own regions.

A second policy decision determined that artists would be selected directly, rather than through a competition procedure. This rationale ultimately reflects the character of the collection as a whole. Cinemas are, for the most part, community oriented centres, drawing their audiences from well-defined areas. The Art Program is, like every other aspect of the company's corporate image, one over which Cineplex Odeon must exercise close control. Each work of art must be chosen with regard both to the geographical location as well as the design and character of each cinema. A further, and probably the most significant factor, is that many artists—including some of the best—will not submit proposals to competitions. We do not want the Program to lose artists for this reason.

Typically, the selection procedure begins with my wife Marilyn and I consulting with David Mesbur, President of David K. Mesbur Architect Ltd., on the design of a particular building and the possible siting for a work of art. We must ensure that the works of art have prominent places in the buildings—invariably they become the focal points of the main lobbies. We then make recommendations of artists to Mr. Drabinsky for his decision. Artists selected are then approached with the offer of a commission. There have been a few cases where, for individual reasons, it has not been possible to commission an artist who has been selected to produce a new work. In those instances we have acquired an existing piece for installation. The construction and installation of all works of art are such that they can be removed from the buildings should that necessity arise.

Critical to any program of this sort are the following issues: how the subjects and themes are decided; what expectations are held by the artist and the client; and how the procedures for the client's approval of the work are devised. The Art Program was initiated with the purpose of acquiring works of art of the highest standard that are characteristic of the styles and approaches the artists have developed. As professionals in their field, the subjects of their commissioned works, the approaches taken and the relationship their work bears to the sites, are their decisions. Initial approval of an artist's proposal is made on the basis of a maquette or plan. A process of continuing approval exists in the course of the work's preparation. The Art Program is designed to form a collection of art. Freedom in the creative development of the commissions is a vital function of the quality.

In looking through the pages of this book, the reader will be struck by two important characteristics: first, the breadth and range of the works of art coupled with the decisive individuality of each piece; and second, the emphasis on two-dimensional and low-relief work. There are practical and aesthetic reasons for stressing two-dimensional or low-relief works. With space in the cinemas at a premium, and with the need to ensure both the free movement of people through the lobbies and security for the art, wall-mounted pieces that do not intrude physically into the theatre space are necessary. In some buildings, the sites for art are such that they allow relief work and a number of artists, including Charles Gagnon, Richard Mill, Gordon Rayner, Jack Shadbolt, Harold Town and Alan Wood have chosen to make relief paintings or painted constructions. The character and configuration of the lobby at the Spectrum Cinemas in Houston, not only allowed for, but suggested a sculptural rather than a painted work—for this reason the commission was offered to John Noestheden.

In the past sixty or seventy years there has been a profound and mutual influence between film and painting. The Art Program is an opportunity to form a collection that directly and indirectly investigates the relationship between the arts: their parallels and contrasts; their differing structures of unity and illusion; and their development of visual languages.

Some artists have chosen to respond explicitly to the theme of movies—John Hall, Gordon Rayner, Phil Richards, Joyce Wieland, Alan Wood and Gerald Zeldin are among them. Others have done so indirectly—this is true, in widely differing ways, of Charles Gagnon, Gathie Falk, Doug Haynes, Richard Mill and Paul Fournier. A further level of contact exists in the way that many painters use photography in the process of developing their paintings. This may be structural, as with Christian Knudsen and Will Gorlitz, or where photographs are used as direct sources—such is the case of John Hall's and David Thauberger's paintings and of Harold Town's THE FAMOUS drawings. For some artists— Yves Gaucher, Robert Scott, Ulysse Comtois, Otto Rogers and Vicky Marshall, to mention a few—the very character of their work precludes their seeking a direct response to movies in their paintings. At the core, in every case, is the way that the artists respond as individuals to the situations presented to them. Their responses are their statements, the cinema setting gives context to stimulate and provoke reaction.

The freedom realized in the artist's responses bears on the way that the Art Program establishes a relationship between cinema architecture and the visual arts in a form quite distinct from the prevailing tradition. Many of us recall, with a warm sense of nostalgia, the great movie palaces of our childhood and youth. They were, in their grandeur and extravagance, magical places. But many people in today's audiences have no such memories. When they began going to movies, those grand old buildings had either fallen into disuse, or suffered under crude surgery. The passing of those buildings reflected changing patterns not only in the demand for entertainment but, broadly, in social life. At one time, whole communities patronized the local, single-screen cinema. Audiences are now seeking a wider choice of movies in response to their diverse interests. And those old buildings were curious not only in the way they existed for a modern form of entertainment — the movies — but for their architectural

style, which sought to emulate the traditions of theatre and opera houses. In those contexts, art was used most often as a function of decoration.

The approach Cineplex Odeon has taken in building its cinemas — that is, the way in which space is used and the ambience created — responds to the new patterns of moviegoing. The Art Program was, therefore, developed in ways to complement the character and the use of the buildings. It seeks not only to emphasize the contemporary in art, but to encompass its range and individuality, giving it a place where it exists for its own sake, rather than as an adjunct to the architecture. One of our decisions was that we would use the work of Canadian artists both for cinemas in Canada and the United States. This was appropriate not only because Cineplex Odeon is a Canadian corporation, but also because, with its broad business reach, the Corporation's support of the visual arts could make an important contribution to spreading recognition of the excellence in Canadian art, not only across the country but also beyond its borders. This has special importance for Canada whose artistic traditions are largely based in nineteenth century European models and

where the emergence of modernist art is so recent that it is, in part, described by the early careers of such artists as Jack Shadbolt, Harold Town and William Ronald.

In this age of mass communication and travel, knowledge of what is happening in the art world, nationally and internationally, is rapidly disseminated. Yet, the art that is known and circulated internationally accounts for only a small fraction of what is produced. Art remains a very particular, individual activity. Its essence lies in the expression of the artist and his or her way of life rather than in generalizations of styles and movements. This tension between the internationalism of art and the work of individual artists is not, however, a neutralizing balance but rather the very impetus out of which dispute, change and development arise. The Art Program, in giving continuing support to artists in the regions where they live and by broadcasting their work outside those regions, contributes to the dynamics of that vital tension. The support that the Program gives to the arts in Canada is rewarded by the calibre of art it encourages and the unique character of the collection Cineplex Odeon is building.

David Burnett

Gerald Gladstone, <u>LIFE FORCE</u>, 1982.
Beverly Center Cinemas,
Los Angeles (Beverly Hills), California.

11

ASPELL

Peter Aspell was for many years a teacher of art: at the Vancouver School of Art from 1948-70; thereafter, until 1978 he ran his own school. He also taught for twenty years in the Extension Department of the University of British Columbia. Until the later 1970s he exhibited abstract works, principally in group shows. He made a long series of paintings based on the formal structure of the T. At the same time he began to make figure and still-life paintings. During the next few years figurative paintings gradually became dominant.

For many years his work was little recognized outside of Vancouver; but his recent work has gained a great deal of attention through one-man exhibitions in Vancouver, Toronto, Los Angeles, New York, and Paris.

Aspell's work is a bridge that links an interest in the art and traditions of past cultures with an energetic, vital urge for expression. He describes this as the need to 'go back to...primordial instincts and time to get at...something inside us which through civilization and the glossing over of civilization we lose'.[*]

POND MAGIC is one of a group of paintings with the same title. The image is that of the past lying layered but undiminished in potential beneath stilled waters. The inspiration for his images come from many sources: artifacts of ancient African cultures, the Indians of the North West Coast and the paintings of such artists as Paul Klee and Chaim Soutine. Aspell's particular admiration of Velazquez is expressed in his richly layered colours and dense, painterly textures.

[*]*In PETER ASPELL PAINTINGS
New York: Gallery Moos.
October 1987.*

---

*b. Vancouver, British Columbia: 1918.
Studied at the Vancouver School of Art, Vancouver;
and Academie de Ghent, Belgium.
Lives in Vancouver, British Columbia.*

*Painting installed December 1988.
Marina MarketPlace Cinemas,
Los Angeles (Marina del Rey), California.*

6. <u>POND MAGIC</u>, 1987-88.
Oil on canvas.
2.13 x 6.10 metres,
(7 x 20 feet).

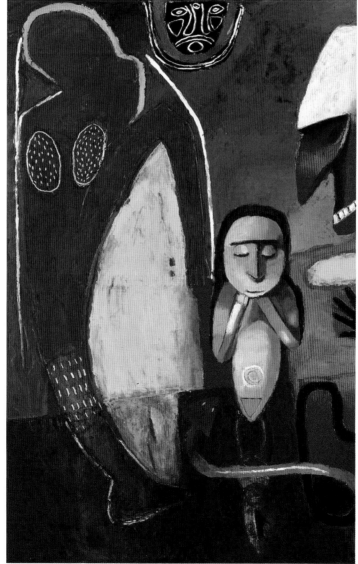

Detail.

BACHINSKI

Walter Bachinski's artistic interests and concerns are set firmly in the classical tradition, the approach to pictorial representation which has been at the core of Western art since the Renaissance. This tradition has been engaged and reinterpreted by each succeeding generation of artists and in this century its most profound interpreters have been Picasso and Matisse.

In acknowledging these modern masters, Bachinski, a professor of drawing and print-making at the University of Guelph for more than twenty years, has sought to create a distinctive style. This is found in his drawings, pastels and sculptures, where the human figure has been his most frequent subject.

PASTORAL is in six contiguous sections and is created with pastels on a heavy rag paper. Bachinski has used dance, the central theme of the work, as a metaphor of the movement and rhythm of film. The left-hand sections of the picture contain a harlequin and a girl playing the panpipes, an evocation of the music that is crucial to film construction. The two sections on the right show still-life elements in an interior setting. Bachinski describes these as a "variable setting." The elements represent physical changes and movement in the process of film-making – changes of scene, camera angles, and editing cuts.

Pastel is a dry-paste mixture of ground pigments and gum-water compressed in a crayon form. The pastel technique produces colours of special brilliance and delicacy. To ensure a strong, permanent bond between the material and the paper, the finished work has been fixed with an acrylic solution. PASTORAL has been covered with Den-glass, a non-reflecting glass that protects the surface of the work without distorting its colour or texture.

b. Ottawa, Ontario: 1939.
Graduated from the Ontario College of Art, Toronto, 1965.
MA, University of Iowa, Iowa City, 1967.
Lives in Guelph, Ontario.

Painting installed July 1988.
Fairway Cinemas, Kitchener, Ontario.

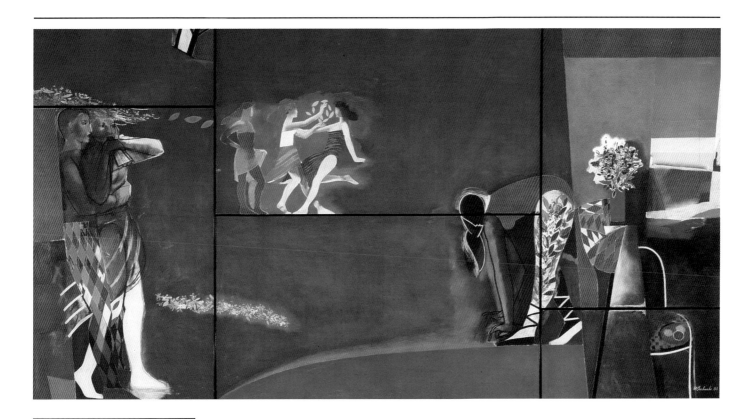

7. <u>PASTORAL</u>, 1988.
Pastel on paper.
2.44 x 4.57 metres,
(8 x 15 feet).

Detail.

BOLDUC

The critic Barrie Hale has identified three generations of Toronto modernist painters. The first generation was represented by the Painters Eleven group formed in 1953 and the second generation centred on the 'Isaacs group' artists (see p. 76). Hale described David Bolduc's work as forming a bridge between the second and third generations of painters who began to exhibit in the 1970s.*

Bolduc's work is vibrant in colour and his paint handling is expressive. His subjects, based on objects or landscape, are 'abstracted' rather than abstract. In contrast to the works of his contemporaries – for example, the 'all-over' character of Paul Hutner's paintings (see p. 52), or the constructions of Paul Sloggett (see p. 94) – Bolduc's paintings tend towards central, vertical images, reminiscent of plants or leaves or fans. These images are drawn in veins of pure colour and are placed on wide, inflected fields of colour.

MADISON BLUES wittily and ingeniously establishes compositional rhythm in a work sited in a relatively narrow space where it is most commonly viewed from the side. This painting is in five sections, each carrying central emblematic images surrounded by crosses and set in fields of different colours and textures. The impact of each image is played against a sense of panorama. This effect is exaggerated by both the internal structure and the dimensions of the work: the sections diminish in size from the centre. However, to prevent us from merely scanning the work, he reverses the perspectival flow in the second panel from the left, stopping us from moving along and encouraging us to confront the picture head on.

Bolduc's interest in the process and structure of collage is reflected in the structure and composition of his paintings. The design of the Madison Cinemas provides an ideal opportunity to showcase Bolduc's collages. Five of these works are installed in the café adjacent to the theatre lobby.

*Barrie Hale 'Out of the Park. Modernist Painting in Toronto, 1950-1980' PROVINCIAL ESSAYS VOL 2, 1985. p. 81.

b. Toronto, Ontario: 1945.
Studied at the Ontario College of Art, Toronto, 1963-64 and the Montréal Museum of Fine Arts, School of Art and Design, Montréal, 1965-66.
Lives in Toronto, Ontario.

Paintings and five works on paper installed October 1986.
Madison Cinemas, Toronto (North York), Ontario.

8. <u>MADISON BLUES</u>, 1986.
Acrylic on canvas.
Five parts; 2.44 x 7.62 metres,
(8 x 25 feet) overall.

Detail.

BOYER

Bob Boyer is a Metis artist and teacher. In 1978 he joined the faculty of the Saskatchewan Indian Federated College in Regina. Since 1980 he has been Head of the Department of Indian Art at the College.

Boyer's paintings integrate formal painterly qualities with the structure and meaning of Plains Indian design. He has expressed a desire 'to put Indian spiritual concepts back into the work,'* not in a simple revival or renewal of Plains artifacts but through personal interpretations of historical and contemporary events by means of the traditions of Indian iconography.

Boyer's paintings incorporate powerful colour and strong geometric structure. They are formal, abstract works of art, yet they also derive meaning from the presence of traditional forms of Plains beadwork design and hide painting. Since 1983, Boyer has made many of his paintings on blankets, echoing the teepee liners that were attached to the insides of traditional Plains dwellings.

The design of the Coronet Cinemas lent itself to two separate paintings. Resonating along the length of the lobby are THE MOUNTAINS, THE NIGHT AND THE 49 installed in the main section of the lobby and 10 MINUTES TO DRUM ROLL CALL, a diptych, at the far end of the lobby.

*Karen Duffek 'Bob Boyer: A Blanket Statement' UBC MUSEUM OF ANTHROPOLOGY MUSEUM NOTE NO. 23. 1988.

b. Prince Albert, Saskatchewan: 1948.
BEd, University of Saskatchewan, 1971.
Lives in Regina, Saskatchewan.

Paintings installed March 1988.
Coronet Cinemas, Regina, Saskatchewan.

9. <u>TEN MINUTES TO DRUM ROLL CALL</u>, 1988. *(left)*
Oil and beeswax over acrylic on canvas.
Two parts; 1.52 x 3.05 metres,
(5 x 10 feet) overall.

10. <u>THE MOUNTAINS, THE NIGHT AND THE 49</u>, 1988. *(below)*
Oil and beeswax over acrylic on canvas.
2.13 x 3.05 metres, (7 x 10 feet).

BROADHURST

Still-life and landscape – intimate reflections of his immediate surroundings – are the subjects of Christopher Broadhurst's paintings. He expresses these portrayals in surfaces of heavy impasto and layers of rich, strong colour. Trained as a printmaker, he is largely self-taught as a painter. He has, until recently, taught painting at Queen's University, both at the Agnes Etherington Art Centre and the Department of Fine Art.

In this commission, Broadhurst wanted to refer to filmic structure without an approach that would involve pointed narration. The triptych form of A DAY OF SUMMER RAIN alludes to the linear frame sequence of film while introducing the theme of time and movement in landscape. Each panel refers to a particular time of day, and there is a rhythm across the picture corresponding to a sequence of anticipation, action and its aftermath.

The painting is installed on a bulkhead that separates the lobby from the theatres. Because it is viewed from below as one enters the building and crosses the lobby, Broadhurst set the horizon line low. By curving the horizon down from the outer panels towards the centre he extends the illusion of depth, thereby drawing the viewer's attention into the picture.

b. England: 1953.
Moved to Canada, 1954.
BFA, Queen's University,
Kingston, 1977.
Lives in Tamworth, Ontario.
Paintings installed October 1986.
Cataraqui Cinemas,
Kingston, Ontario.

11. <u>A DAY OF SUMMER RAIN</u>, 1986.
Oil on canvas.
Three parts; 1.68 x 6.40 metres,
(5.5 x 21 feet) overall.

Detail.

BURNETT

Advanced art in Toronto during the later 1970s appeared to be dominated by installation sculpture, video art and abstract painting. However, at that time, too, a number of young painters decided to challenge that primacy. Their painting was figurative and tough in subject matter. The drawing was often raw and their handling of paint loaded and expressive. In 1981 a group of these artists, among them Brian Burnett, formed an artist-run gallery called CHROMAZONE. During its short existence, the gallery quickly gained critical attention, broadened the debate on art in the city and introduced a direction for new art in Toronto that responded to similar developments occurring in Europe.

Brian Burnett has invariably taken as his theme the environments in which he has lived and worked. His paintings are interpretations of places, capturing their mood and spirit, whether in neighbourhoods of Toronto, the forests on the British Columbia coast or in the city of Berlin. In many of his earlier paintings, Burnett would paint disembodied eyes on the buildings as if to show the reciprocity between his viewpoint and that of his subjects.

Burnett lived in Windsor as a child. In BRIDGE TO THE UNIVERSE he expressed his sense of returning to the city. The painting is a series of superimposed frames, establishing the position of the city on a map of North America and centering the image on the skyline and the bridge over the Detroit River, as if approaching it from the East.

b. South Porcupine, Ontario: 1952.
Studied at the New School of Art, Toronto, 1974-75.
Lives in Toronto, Ontario.

Painting installed November 1987.
Palace Cinemas, Windsor, Ontario.

12. <u>BRIDGE TO THE UNIVERSE</u>, 1987.
Acrylic on canvas.
Irregular; 3.04 x 3.96 metres,
(10 x 13 feet).

CLARK

For a short period at the beginning of his career, John Clark experimented with abstract painting. He abandoned this, believing that it was still possible to make new figurative art of high quality – a difficult decision for a young painter to make in the late 1960s. He was impressed by the work of the American painter Edward Hopper and his own painting reflects something of Hopper's sense of the alienation of people in urban surroundings. The figures Clark paints, however, have nothing of Hopper's complacency – they are assertive, sometimes protesting, often heroic. The fragmented narratives in Clark's work, the unsettling perspectives and simple, powerfully described elements have something of a comic-strip character. But to say this does not take into account Clark's painterly touch. He has a particularly sensitive and authoritative control of painterly structure – a technique of short, emphatic brush-strokes that bring both drawing and painting to a single structure of representation.

THE RIVER is a painting in two parts, one echoing the other. The subject has an immediate, local reference – to the Oldman River beside which Lethbridge stands. The river has long been vital to the indigenous people of the region. The painting expresses their concerns, and the concerns of others to environmental threats. The linked images of the uprooted tree and the spread-eagled man carried down the river seem to reflect both disaster and powerlessness. At the same time, however, they represent a unity of forces, natural and cultural, that seek to deny destruction.

b. Yorkshire, England: 1943.
Moved to Canada, 1978.
Graduated from the Hull College
of Art, Hull, England, 1965.
MFA, Indiana University, 1968.
Lives in Lethbridge, Alberta.

Painting installed August 1988.
Park Place Cinemas,
Lethbridge, Alberta.

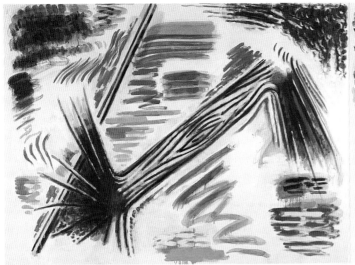

13. <u>THE RIVER</u>, 1988.
Oil and acrylic on canvas.
Two parts; 1.83 x 4.88 metres,
(6 x 16 feet) overall.

Detail.

COMTOIS

After an unsatisfying year of formal art studies, Ulysse Comtois began painting independently; he joined the young artists of the avant-garde in Montréal who grouped themselves around Paul-Emile Borduas and the Automatiste movement. Comtois' early work was similar to that of many of his contemporaries – abstract paintings, 'automatic' in concept and gestural in style. During the 1950s, as part of a broad revision in approach among advanced painters in Montréal, Comtois' work took on a more geometric character. In 1960, he extended the logic of that direction in his first sculptures.

For ten years, beginning in 1964, Comtois concentrated on sculpture. At first he emphasized complex forms made of laminated wood which he painted. A logical extension of this work involved units of machine-formed aluminium stacked around a pole so that each element swivelled individually. These works, having no fixed form but an infinite range of positions, could be formed and reformed time and again.

In the mid-1970s Comtois returned to painting; the cool geometry of the aluminium sculptures gave way to 'all-over' abstractions, brilliantly coloured in a pointillist-like technique. His most recent work retains the coloured-dot technique but is explicitly representational, with a particular emphasis on landscape. AUTUMN MORNING, inspired by early morning walks near his home, is the most ambitious work in this latest development of Comtois' career.

b. Granby, Québec: 1931.
Studied at the Ecole des
beaux-arts, Montréal, 1948.
Lives in Ste-Madeleine, Québec.

Painting installed December 1988.
River Oaks Cinemas 1-6,
Chicago (Calumet City), Illinois.

14. <u>AUTUMN MORNING</u>, 1988.
Oil and acrylic on panel.
2.13 x 4.88 metres, (7 x 16 feet).

Detail.

DARRAH

A major factor in the development of modernist art in Alberta and Saskatchewan has been the Workshops held each year at Emma Lake in Northern Saskatchewan. Jack Shadbolt (see p. 90) led the first of these Workshops in 1955. Subsequently many Workshop leaders have been major New York painters and sculptors, including Barnet Newman, Jules Olitski, Kenneth Noland, Larry Poons and Michael Steiner. The abstract formalist character of the work of so many of these leaders has had a significant impact on many prairie artists. In Edmonton, for example, a substantial group of formalist painters and sculptors are a strong artistic force.

Phil Darrah's work is characterized by broad sweeps of colour across stained grounds. Sometimes he uses rectangular fields; at other times he investigates the formal tensions created by radically shaped canvases. So determinedly abstract an approach does not lend itself easily to narrative or metaphor. In developing the composition for WESTERN PROJECTIONS, Darrah saw the diagonals of the painting as references to the expanding wedge of light emanating from a projector. A more significant correspondence to him, however, between film and painting, is in the shared interest in changing qualities of light, and transparency of colour.

b. England: 1940.
Moved to Canada, 1970.
Graduated from the Slade School of
Fine Art, London, 1964.
Lives in Edmonton, Alberta.

Painting installed November 1985.
West Mall 8 in West Edmonton Mall,
Edmonton, Alberta.

15. <u>WESTERN PROJECTIONS</u>, 1985.
Acrylic on canvas.
2.29 x 8.53 metres, (7.5 x 28 feet).

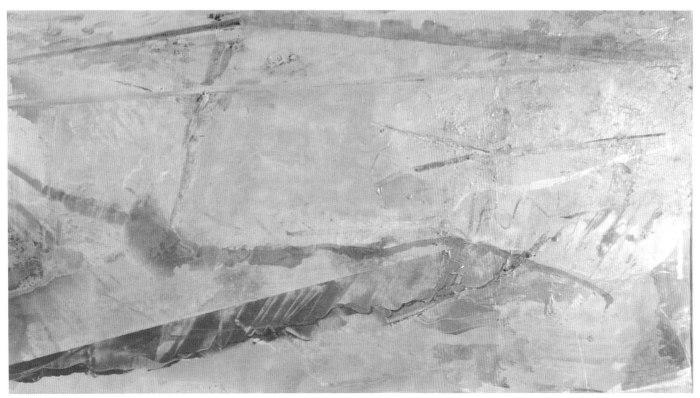

Detail.

DRAPELL

As a teenager Joseph Drapell took art lessons, but his wish to enter art school was denied by the Czechoslovakian education authorities who wanted to produce engineers, not artists. After graduating as a chemist, he worked as a set painter at the National Theatre in Prague. In 1965 he defected while on a holiday in Austria and made his way to Canada.

While studying at the Cranbrook Academy, he met the painter Jack Bush and the art critic Clement Greenberg. Both men became major influences on the direction of his work and the self-discipline he brought to its development. During the 1970s Drapell began to develop his personal response to abstract painting. Despite the vitality of his abstract imagery, however, he could not, nor would not jettison the references to the outside world that affect the colour and structure of his paintings. Landscape, and in particular the island-studded waters of Georgian Bay, has been a constant inspiration and in recent years many of his paintings have undertaken explicit responses to it.

Early in the 1970s he developed a painting technique in which he swept a length of wood in arcs or circles through fresh paint laid over dried, ground layers. The result was dynamic, radiating images in complex glowing colour. In 1983 he developed a variant of this technique, using an aluminium bar into which he had cut grooves, rather like a comb. This would produce a relief surface with alternate areas of smooth and ridged paint. In FILM POWER he takes the process further still, creating complex billowing sweeps across the surface that leave high, thick ridges of paint. In addition he used interference paint that reflects ambient light differently as the spectator changes position, producing expanded and dynamic colour effects.

b. Humpolec, Czechoslovakia: 1940.
Moved to Canada, 1965.
MFA Cranbrook Academy,
Bloomfield Hills, Michigan, 1970.
Lives in Toronto, Ontario.

Painting installed August 1986.
Promenade Cinemas,
Toronto (Thornhill), Ontario

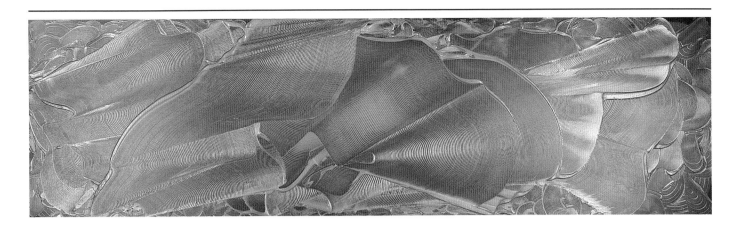

16. <u>FILM POWER</u>, 1986.
Acrylic on canvas.
2.13 x 7.62 metres,
(7 x 25 feet).

Detail.

EWEN

In recent years the paintings of Paterson Ewen have drawn a great deal of critical attention. In 1987 a travelling exhibition of his early work was organized by the Mendel Art Gallery in Regina and in the same year a major survey exhibition of his paintings of the past twenty years was organized by the Art Gallery of Ontario and toured across Canada.

Ewen's work can be divided into several distinct phases: the early figurative work in the 1950s gave way to a style of gestural abstraction; later, throughout the 1960s, he concentrated on minimalist abstraction contributing to the issues under debate in advanced art in Montréal. In 1968 he moved from Montréal and settled in London. In 1970 he made the most decisive change in the direction of his work. In the course of hand-gouging a large sheet of plywood, from which he intended to make a woodcut print, he realized that the gouged plywood and applied paint already constituted a finished work.

Since this discovery he has developed and extended this technique, hand-gouging and machine routing sheets of plywood which he then bonds together. He paints these excavated surfaces and often adds other materials, such as metal, leather and wire. The subjects of these works are drawn from his long-held interest in meteorology and natural phenomena: rain and wind storms, storms at sea, the moon and the stars. The raw surfaces of Ewen's paintings, gouged, cut and roughly textured, are brilliant embodiments of the elemental power of their subjects. Moreover, the awesome beauty of nature evinces in Ewen's work an extraordinary subtlety and fineness of response. SUNSET FROM AIRCRAFT (NWT) is a painting of tranquil mood, capturing the delicate sunset colours over the harsh terrain of Northern Canada.

b. Montréal, Québec: 1925. Studied at the Montréal Museum of Fine Arts, School of Art and Design, Montréal, 1948-1950. Lives in London, Ontario.

Painting installed April 1987. Huron Market Place Cinemas, London, Ontario.

17. <u>SUNSET FROM AIRCRAFT (NWT)</u>, 1984.
Acrylic on gouged plywood.
2.44 x 3.35 metres,
(8 x 11 feet).

EYRE

A recent exhibition of Ivan Eyre's figurative paintings at the National Gallery of Canada was entitled <u>PERSONAL MYTHOLOGIES/ IMAGES OF THE MILIEU</u>. 'Personal mythologies' is a loaded phrase which reflects the complex and subtle paintings Eyre has been making for more than thirty years.

He has called his work abstract, despite the figurative, still-life, and landscape images. No matter how his paintings reflect external objects and situations, they remain worlds of their own. He presents to the viewer an essentially ambiguous, visual language, in which meaning oscillates between what we assume to be true of the outside world and what we know to be true of the worlds he creates.

Throughout his career, Eyre has worked simultaneously on figurative subjects, still-life and landscape; sometimes he keeps the genres separate, but as often he combines them. By the end of the 1960s he developed one hybrid structure to which he has returned time and again where the viewer's attention is drawn first to objects set close to us, as if they were gathered on a table. Our gaze then moves past them, as if we were looking through a window, to a landscape beyond. <u>SUNDOWN</u>, painted in 1971, is one of Eyre's earlier paintings of this type. The foreground is filled with a motley collection of objects. They seem familiar, yet – like a word on the tip of the tongue – just beyond description. Objects cast in metal, sheets of paper and pieces of cardboard create an unsettling juxtaposition of weights and textures. Moreover, what seem at first to be buildings beyond the window become ambiguous. They, too, may simply be shapes cut from paper. Only the delicately painted sunset seems to offer a secure identity, but even it leaves us wondering: where, exactly, is the horizon behind which the sun has just sunk?

b. Tullymet, Saskatchewan: 1935.
BFA, University of Manitoba, 1957;
Studied at the University of North Dakota, Grand Forks, 1958-59.
Lives in Winnipeg, Manitoba.

Painting installed September 1988.
900 North Michigan Cinemas, Chicago, Illinois.

18. <u>SUNDOWN</u>, 1971.
Acrylic on canvas.
1.57 x 1.83 metres,
(5.16 x 6 feet).

FALK

Through her work as a sculptor, painter and performance artist, Gathie Falk has given expression to the magic of everyday life, finding wonder in simple objects and events. Art, by giving these objects and events a form separate from their banal contexts, invests them with importance. EIGHT RED BOOTS, of 1973, for example, has eight zip-sided boots in red ceramic displayed in a glass fronted case, while HERD ONE and HERD TWO, of 1974-75 comprise twenty-four painted and drawn plywood cut-out horses, based on the carousel-type horse often found at the entrance to supermarkets. She also made the THERMAL BLANKETS, large, stuffed and quilted canvases on which she painted images derived from snapshots in family photograph albums. In more recent years, she has made paintings of flower beds and of chairs and sofas in garden settings. So often the objects and images in Falk's paintings imply human presence without depicting it.

In 1987, for the Manufacturers Life art billboard project PAINTING THE TOWN, Falk made TWO CURVES CELEBRATING, a semi-circle of white kitchen chairs, each with a bunch of flowers on its seat, set on a semi-circular garden path. She described it as a communion, or a community in readiness, as if seated in a theatre, awaiting a celebratory event. The DEVELOPMENT OF THE PLOT is, to extend that metaphor, cinematic in feeling. It comprises four panels, with the sense of an action developing in sequence across the panels. Some objects are repeated from one panel to the next, others are introduced and then transformed: a fan is shown, it opens, turns into a windmill and then back to a closed fan; a light bulb, first seen as a means of dim illumination, later disappears in a great column of flames.

b. Alexander, Manitoba: 1928.
Studied part-time at the
University of British Columbia,
Vancouver, 1955-63, 1964-67.
Lives in Vancouver, British Columbia.

Painting installed December 1988.
Park and Tilford Cinemas,
Vancouver (North Vancouver), British Columbia.

19. <u>DEVELOPMENT OF THE PLOT</u>,
1988. *Oil on canvas.*
Four parts; 2.13 x 6.10 metres,
(7 x 20 feet) overall.

Detail.

FOURNIER

Paul Fournier is a contemporary of fellow modernist painter David Bolduc (see p. 16). Fournier began exhibiting in Toronto in 1963, and the then well established Toronto painters William Ronald (see below p. 84), Richard Gorman and, above all, Graham Coughtry had an acknowledged influence on his early work. Fournier is best known for his colour-field abstract paintings. However, from time to time, he has turned away from abstraction to make several series of landscape or seascape paintings. (A 1983 exhibition of such works, for instance, was entitled SAILS, SEA, SHELLS AND SHORE.)

Music has played an important, often decisive role in Fournier's creative process, and he describes music 'as a catalyst for invention.' In 1982 he collaborated with the composer Robert Daigneault on an exhibition they entitled BRIDGES, which comprised Fournier's paintings and Daigneault's music.

It was natural, therefore, that Fournier should approach the Cineplex Odeon commission through music. He turned to the film work of John Horner, who composed the scores for STAR TREK II and COCOON, and acknowledged the source of his inspiration by entitling his painting FOR COMPOSER JOHN HORNER. The painting builds through a freely developed rhythm of complex layers accented with areas of bright pure colour: the abstract visual structure evokes the abstract forms of music.

b. Simcoe, Ontario: 1939.
Studied at McMaster University,
Hamilton, 1967-68.
Lives in Unionville, Ontario.

Painting installed August 1986.
Centre Mall Theatres,
Hamilton, Ontario.

20. <u>FOR COMPOSER JOHN HORNER</u>, 1986.
Acrylic on canvas.
2.44 x 6.10 metres,
(8 x 20 feet).

Detail.

GAGNON

Charles Gagnon is a painter, photographer, film-maker and designer of sound installations. In his refusal to concentrate on one medium, he distanced himself from the painting vogues and theoretical arguments dominating Montréal during the 1950s and 1960s. His decisive formative years were those from 1955 to 1960 that were spent in New York, studying, looking at art, painting, and photographing.

There is a complex interplay of photography and painting in Gagnon's work. Their common properties, such as framing devices and methods of illusionism, also differentiate them. Moreover, the ways we understand their realities – the image in a photograph,

the surface in a painting – both coincide and contradict each other. Gagnon's paintings present ambiguities and tensions; their images may allude to windows, yet they will be independent, box-like objects: the illusion of openness is juxtaposed with the reality of enclosure. Some of the paintings are like frames within frames; others are divided like the frames of a film, their two-dimensional structures contrasting with the rich, painterly surfaces that evoke extension into space.

Throughout his career, Gagnon has used words and lettering in his works. For example, in 1972, he won a commission for the External Affairs Building in Ottawa,

dedicated to Lester B. Pearson; he stencilled the words of a Pearson speech onto the paintings. This union of stencilled words and painted surfaces recurs in the Faubourg painting. The format, like a split-screen, is marked with the words 'Transition,' 'Illusion' and 'Refle$_{ct}^{x}$ion,' words that describe the character traits common to film and painting, but which switch in meaning as we shift our attention from one context to another.

*b. Montréal, Québec: 1934.
Studied at the Parsons' School
of Art and Design, 1955-57
and the New York School
of Design, 1957-58.
Lives in Montréal, Québec.*

*Painting installed December 1986.
Cinémas Le Faubourg,
Montréal, Québec.*

21. *Installation of*
TRANSITION/ILLUSION/REFLE$_{CT}^{X}$ION
in the lobby of Cinémas Le Faubourg.

22. <u>TRANSITION/ILLUSION/REFLE</u>_{CT}^X<u>ION</u>, 1986.
Oil on canvas mounted on plywood.
3.12 x 4.11 x .61 metres,
(10.25 x 13.5 x 2 feet).

GAUCHER

After leaving L'Ecole des Beaux-Arts, Yves Gaucher concentrated on print-making. This culminated in 1963, in a suite of embossed prints EN HOMMAGE À WEBERN, a response to the music of Anton Webern.

Gaucher turned to painting in 1964, making rigorously formal, geometric canvases. He maintained the parallels between the temporal rhythms of music and the spatial rhythms in painting. These formal expressions of life's rhythms appeared in a series of paintings entitled DANSES CAREES, (square dances), SIGNALS/SILENCES, and RAGAS, (a Hindu melodic form, the Sanskrit word literally meaning 'colour' or 'mood'). At the end of the 1960s he made a group of grey on grey paintings, works of exceptional subtlety. The viewer becomes absorbed by their slowly revealed spatial rhythms, produced by a series of short horizontal lines in shades of grey set on a grey ground.

In the 1970s Gaucher began making hard-edge, colour field pictures. (Colour field was not only significant to major American painting, but was also at the centre of advanced painting in Montréal.) He used horizontal bands of colour to create a visual balance through the complex rhythms in juxtapositions of hues and tones. In his paintings of the later 1970s, he concentrated on 'the complex problem of the diagonal,' paying homage to late works by the great American painter Barnett Newman. In recent years Gaucher has continued his investigations, concentrating on dark hues. The commission for the Wisconsin Avenue Cinemas, however, offered a specific challenge: creating a work for a strong architectural setting and busy public space. His response was to 'take on the site.' The result is CPX.W, a striking and bold balance of shapes divided between the tonal extremes of black and white and two hues of red.

b. Montréal, Québec: 1934.
Studied at L'Ecole des Beaux-Arts, Montréal, 1956, 1957-60.
Lives in Montréal, Québec.

Painting installed December 1987.
Wisconsin Avenue Cinemas,
Washington, D.C.

23. <u>CPX.W.</u>, 1987.
Acrylic on canvas.
2.29 x 6.10 metres,
(7.5 x 20 feet).

Detail.

GORLITZ

Will Gorlitz explodes the assumption that serious content and fine painting cannot co-exist in contemporary art. He has described his painting HERE WE STAND this way: 'Subject: A flamboyant, colourful tangle of branches of a fruit tree, bearing intermingled apples and pears filling the entire picture plane. Two openings provide views through the tree. Representing relatively small areas of the total picture, the vistas reveal two automobiles.' Gorlitz's phrasing is like the directions in a film script or the stage setting of a play. As we look at the picture, we are waiting for the action to begin. Yet the scene does not easily reveal what might follow. The richly painted tree and the luscious fruit present a conundrum: what conditions are required for apples and pears to be borne by the same tree? Perhaps such a thing is possible only in the Garden of Eden – or in the movies.

The contrast of the fabulous tree and the cars beneath it – the ideal and the commonplace – is paralleled by the way in which we approach the painting. We seem to be viewing the scene from within the branches of the tree. The title, HERE WE STAND, may refer to our viewpoint or to where we must stand in the physical space of the theatre lobby to view the picture. The words may also be declarative rather than descriptive, asserting a position beyond which we will not be forced.

b. Buenos Aires, Argentina: 1952.
Studied University of Manitoba School of Art, 1972-75;
BFA, Nova Scotia College of Art and Design, Halifax, 1977.
Lives in Wellington, Ontario.

Painting installed December 1988.
Fairview Cinemas,
Toronto (North York), Ontario.

24. <u>HERE WE STAND</u>, 1988.
Oil on canvas.
1.52 x 6.71 metres,
(5 x 22 feet).

Detail.

HALL

Traditionally, a still-life painting was a *memento mori*, an image that reminded one of life's brevity. It tended to concentrate on such natural objects as flowers and butterflies, which embodied short-lived beauty, or objects that aroused pleasurable but fleeting senses. John Hall is a painter of still-life, but he is responsive to the late twentieth century view. Our images of nature are so often processed, particularly through photography; our lives seem to be characterized not by natural things but by the man-made objects we collect.

Hall began his career as an abstract painter but found a new direction through the work of American Pop artists of the 1960s – such as the work of Andy Warhol, Jasper Johns and Robert Rauschenberg. Through the 1970s Hall developed paintings that were loaded in their subject matter, sharp in their presentation, and aggressive in their images. Objects from the natural world are pressed into uncomfortable relationships with cheap modern materials while the natural world is transformed into tacky postcards and cheap souvenirs. His photo-realist style emphasizes surfaces and their textures, forcing one to reflect on what it means to conceal our true natures beneath material surfaces.

The Hollywood movie industry – with its dreams and awards, its star system, its contrasts between public achievements and private tragedies – is the subject of Hall's painting RAINBOW. It is a *tableau* of the public faces of the stars, as represented in stills from their films. They are set between Oscars, the symbol of the ultimate Hollywood achievement. The stars are placed against a rich sunset, more the creation of a set painter than nature. It is a still-life for our times, our unique creation of dreams and immortality.

b. Edmonton, Alberta: 1943.
Studied at the Alberta College of Art, 1960-65;
and the Instituto Allende, Mexico, 1965-66.
Lives in Calgary, Alberta.
Chelsea Cinema,
New York, New York.

25. <u>RAINBOW</u>, 1988.
Acrylic on canvas.
1.98 x 5.18 metres,
(6.5 x 17 feet).

Detail.

HARDY

A landscape of wide, low horizons and panoramas unbroken by extensive stands of trees seems an intractable subject for painting. However, landscape painting in Saskatchewan has a substantial history. Moreover, successive generations of artists have developed a distinctive stylistic approach. This tradition originated early in the century with such painters as Inglis Sheldon-Williams and Augustus Kenderdine, who sought to adapt their training in the English School of landscape painting to their new environment. These beginnings were broadened and developed by a number of artists, notably the Saskatoon painters Ernst Lindner, Wynona Mulcaster, Reta Cowley, and Dorothy Knowles.

Perhaps the decisive influence on this development was that of the succession of artists who have been leaders at the Emma Lake Workshops (see above p.28). Although most of those leaders have been abstract painters, the example of their work, particularly in their approach to light and colour and their emphasis on painterly freedom has had a marked effect on the landscape painters. Greg Hardy attended a number of the Workshops in the late 1970s and early 1980s and went on to become one of the leading artists among a younger generation of Saskatchewan landscape painters. Unlike the approaches of earlier landscape painters, characterized by thin layers of colour unified by the lightness of the underpainting, Hardy's work has moved towards a richer level of colour and a heavier impasto as a response to the intensity and clarity of light that is the special character of the Prairie landscape.

b. Saskatoon, Saskatchewan: 1950.
Studied at Ryerson Polytechnical Institute, Toronto, 1970-72.
Lives in Meacham, Saskatchewan.

Bricktown Square Cinemas, Chicago, Illinois.

26. <u>PRAIRIE MARSH</u>, 1988.
Oil on canvas.
1.98 x 5.03 metres,
(6.5 x 16.5 feet).

Detail.

HAYNES

For some years Doug Haynes has been a leading figure among the colour-abstractionist painters of Edmonton. His influence is two-fold – in his work and through his teaching at the University of Alberta since 1969. His paintings have evolved through a number of structural and colouristic transformations. However, each stage has been an exploration of the formal abstract tensions between shape and colour, the integrity of the painted surface and its illusion of depth.

In 1985 Haynes held an exhibition of his paintings, 'Cubism Re-Visited,' at the Edmonton Art Gallery. The works re-evaluated, in terms of his own earlier work, the move towards abstraction in the early Cubist paintings of Braque and Picasso. It is a continuation of these investigations that became the basis of the commissioned Westmount painting 40S HEROES AND WIDE, WIDE 50S. The paintings are structured with the overlapping planes of colour characteristic of Analytic Cubism. However his point of reference is the abstract painting of recent years rather than the Cubists' abstraction from figure or still-life subjects.

In 40S HEROES AND WIDE, WIDE 50S Haynes applies his painterly approach to a particular historical aspect of film. His painting is divided into two parts: the left side – square, painted in black and white – refers to the format and presentation of films of the 1940s. The right side – broader in proportion, more colourful and more active – refers to the changes in movie-making techniques and presentation that characterized the 1950s.

b. Regina, Saskatchewan: 1936.
Graduated from the Alberta
College of Art, Calgary, 1958.
Lives in Edmonton, Alberta.
Painting installed November 1985.
Westmount Cinemas,
Edmonton, Alberta.

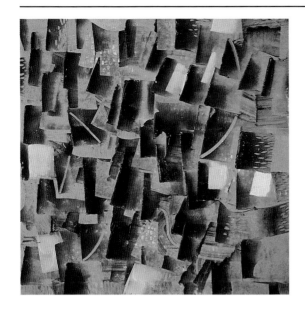 

27. <u>40S HEROES AND WIDE,</u>
<u>WIDE 50S</u>, 1985.
Acrylic on canvas.
Two parts; '40s Heroes'
2.06 x 2.06 metres, (6.75 x 6.75 feet);
'Wide, Wide 50s'
2.06 x 2.31 metres, (6.75 x 7.58 feet).

Detail.

HUTNER

Painting in Toronto since the 1950s has shown a bias towards high keyed colour, expressionistic drawing and figurative or objective images. Paul Hutner's paintings, vibrant in colour and richly layered, are at the centre of this tradition. Hutner invariably works by a process of theme and variations, developing a series of paintings which begin from a particular reference point. He has, for instance, made a series based on flags, another on maps and yet another on words.

At the time that he received the Cineplex Odeon commission, Hutner had been using masks as his underlying structure. His interest in masks (as it had been in flags and maps) lay not only in their objective meanings, but also in their character of abstraction.

Taking the drama of film as his specific task for this commission, he began with the traditional masks of Tragedy and Comedy. Reducing these to sharply cut triangles with large oval eyeholes, he used their geometry as the basis for the Hillsboro Cinemas paintings. Using these masks as both the formal structure and the point of reference for their images, the paintings were built freely in layer on layer of colour and drawing. In the process of working, and without concealing their origins, the paintings became abstract expressions of Hutner's experience of the Florida landscape, as he keyed his colours to the blues of the ocean and the richly varied flora of the region.

The wide, symmetrically planned lobby of the Hillsboro Cinemas with its central concession stand led to the decision to have Hutner paint two canvases equal in size and complementary in theme. Hence CRUISIN' #1 and CRUISIN' #2 are installed facing each other across the lobby.

b. Toronto, Ontario 1948.
Studied at the New School of Art, Toronto, 1967 - 69.
Lives in Toronto, Ontario.

Paintings installed March 1988.
Hillsboro Cinemas, Tampa, Florida.

KIRTON

By his mid-twenties, Doug Kirton had already attracted the attention of critics and collectors. At that time his paintings comprised single objects – a bedstead, a staircase, a curtain – isolated on a flat plane. He emphasized the direct simplicity of these images by limiting his colours and painting his surfaces to a smooth, hard finish.

In the mid-1980s he moved away from this approach, further restricted his palette to shades of grey, and took as his subject suburban houses. He based his images on the small, poor-quality, half-tone photographs used by real estate companies in their advertising material.

After three or four years, Kirton radically changed both his images and his painting technique. He began to make landscape paintings, using more open brushwork and a broad range of colour. The images themselves were still based on photographs, like those on picture postcards. These provide an ironic response to the cliché of landscape, the 'natural view' that historically has dominated Canadian painting.

In these landscape paintings Kirton questioned our assumptions about natural beauty, playing them against equally firm notions of what comprises the beautiful in painting. His most recent paintings are a series called TOXIC PONDS, in which he uses the deceptive calm and rich colour often indicative of a natural environment poisoned by industrial pollution. Ironically such subjects do not necessarily restrict the painter. Kirton has developed a rich and sensuous use of colour and a freedom in his handling of paint that make him one of the most striking of young painters. The River-Tree Court at Hawthorn commission, entitled AFTERNOON, provided Kirton with his most ambitious opportunity and challenge.

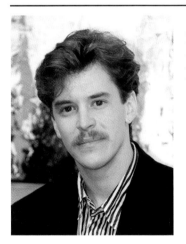

b. London, Ontario: 1955.
BFA, Nova Scotia College of Art and Design, Halifax, 1978.
Lives in Toronto, Ontario.

Painting installed October 1988. RiverTree Court at Hawthorn, Chicago (Vernon Hills), Illinois.

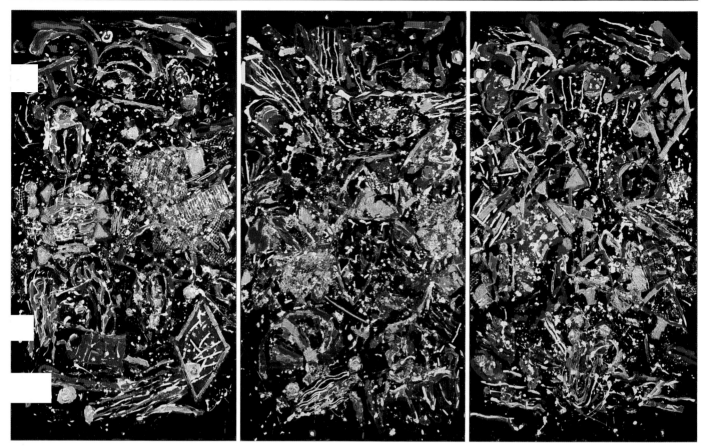

31. <u>HOMAGE TO FELLINI</u>, 1986.
Acrylic paint and mixed
media on canvas.
Three parts; 3.05 x 4.88 metres,
(10 x 16 feet) overall.

JACOBS

In their formation of structure, use of colour, and development of textures, many abstract painters in Canada have used the landscape as a point of inspiration. Often, artists with many years of abstract painting behind them, have turned to make explicit landscape pictures. In contrast, the sense of Katja Jacobs' work is urban. She makes paintings that reflect the life of the street, or the market, or the bazaar. They seem filled with noise and bustle, argument, agreement and activity.

Jacobs trained as a printmaker and the influence of printmaking processes carried through into her paintings. This is apparent in her emphasis on drawing and how she reveals coloured forms by scraping away covering layers and 'stops out' parts of the composition as if she were preparing a printing plate or woodcut for inking.

In her most recent works the element of drawing has become much more a function of her use of colour. At the same time, collage, which has always been a factor in her work, is used more emphatically. She fixes a wide range of materials to her canvases, embedding them into the surface with layers of colour. Jacobs' HOMAGE TO FELLINI, marking her respect for the great Italian film director, is energetic and dynamic. And with its black ground like a night sky, it seems like a flight of fantasy.

b. Germany: 1939. Moved to Canada, 1963.
Studied at Akademie der Bildenden Künste, Freiburg, Germany;
and L'Ecole des Beaux Arts, Brussels, Belgium.
Lives in Toronto, Ontario.

Painting installed June 1986.
South Common Mall Cinemas,
Toronto (Mississauga), Ontario.

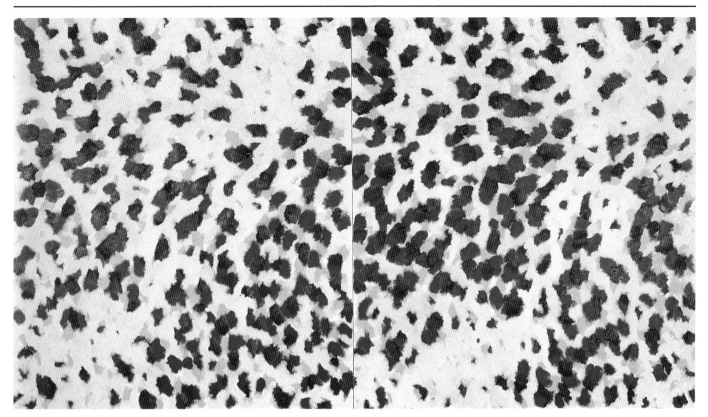

30. <u>HIGHLANDS #3</u>, 1975.
Oil on canvas.
2.13 x 3.05 metres,
(7 x 13 feet).

ISKOWITZ

Gershon Iskowitz's life was one of triumph over tragedy, and his work is an extraordinary witness to that triumph.

With the German invasion of Poland in September 1939, Iskowitz was sent into forced labour. Three years later, during the Nazi 'resettlements,' his family, with the exception of himself and one of his brothers, was taken to the Treblinka concentration camp and put to death. He and his brother continued in forced labour until sent to Auschwitz in September 1943. There, his brother died. A year later Iskowitz was transferred to Buchenwald, where he remained until he was liberated by U.S troops.

He managed to continue his childhood interest in drawing through the war years, and a few works from this period survive. After a long stay in a Munich hospital after the war, Iskowitz began art studies first, for a brief time at the Munich Academy of Art. He later took private lessons with Oskar Kokoschka.

In 1949 he immigrated to Canada and settled in Toronto. His paintings and drawings from his first years in Toronto are almost wholly concerned with the horror of the past and attempt to recreate the family he had lost. Later he began to draw and paint north of Toronto, gradually superseding a literal representation of the landscape by an abstract expression of its colours, light, and movement.

Iskowitz's paintings were radically changed after his experience of a helicopter flight over Northern Manitoba in 1967: swiftly moving across the landscape; rising and falling; catching only impressions of the changing patterns of colours in the trees, lakes and rocks. From that time, in one richly painted surface after another, Iskowitz expressed and re-expressed this experience. These paintings are joyous celebrations of the beauty and freedom of that flight. They reflect the generosity of spirit and openness of their creator, who became a special friend and example for so many younger Toronto artists.

HIGHLANDS NO. 3 was painted in 1975 and acquired for installation in the Marketsquare 4 Cinemas. It is a brilliant example of Iskowitz's art, in its richness, depth of colour and dynamic surface.

b. Kielce, Poland: 1921.
Moved to Canada, 1949.
d. Toronto, Ontario: 1988.

Painting installed July 1987.
Marketsquare 4 Cinemas,
Atlanta (North Decatur), Georgia.

28. <u>CRUISIN' #1</u>, 1988. *(left)*
Acrylic on canvas.
1.83 x 3.05 metres,
(6 x 10 feet)

29. <u>CRUISIN' #2</u>, 1988. *(below)*
Acrylic on canvas.
1.83 x 3.05 metres,
(6 x 10 feet).

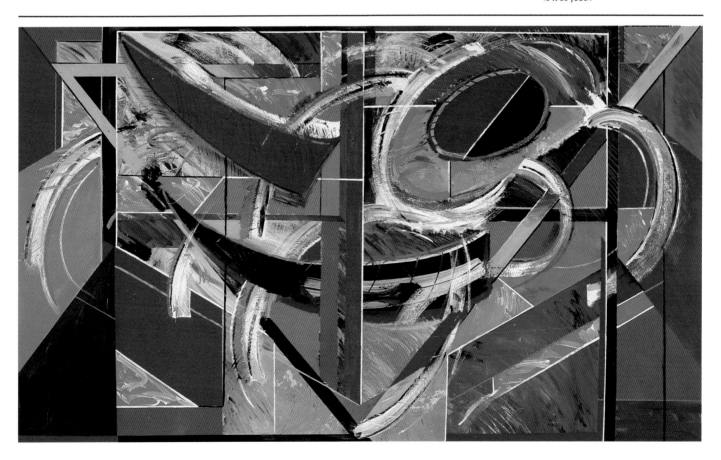

32. <u>AFTERNOON</u>, 1988.
Oil on canvas.
Three parts; 2.44 x 5.49 metres,
(8 x 18 feet) overall.

Detail.

KLUNDER

Harold Klunder is one of the artists who disproved the critical pronouncements of the 1970s that painting was, if not dead, at least fatally ill. Moreover, Klunder showed, and continues to show, the extraordinary capacity of painting to adapt without losing its essence. Central to this is the way in which some painters–Klunder is among them–who have a special sensitivity to the nature of their material. Painters of this sort do not simply make an image but, retain the sense of paint's malleable character. They produce paintings whose forms appear as if they are still fresh from the process of formation.

This sense of process has been central to Klunder's work. His paintings of the 1970s were abstract in image; however, unlike the thin, stain technique popular at the time, Klunder's approach built up the surface in thick layers. A tension exists between the geometric structures of his images and their open, tactile surfaces. Over the years, the dynamic tension in the surfaces seemed first to loosen and then to submerge the geometric forms. In the paintings of the late 1970s and early 1980s, however, the abstract images of texture and colour began to form into discernible figurative forms: suggestions of landscapes and the shapes of heads. Klunder has described these as bringing about a presence, a sense of becoming.

Klunder produces his paintings slowly, working and reworking, gradually building up the surfaces, allowing the images to emerge intuitively. He began painting THE POET'S GARDEN III (SELF PORTRAIT) in 1982 and completed it three years later.

b. Deventer, The Netherlands: 1943.
Moved to Canada, 1951.
Studied at Central Technical School,
Toronto, 1960-1964.
Lives in Flesherton, Ontario.

Painting installed December 1987.
McClurg Court Cinemas,
Chicago, Illinois.

33. <u>THE POET'S GARDEN III</u>
<u>(SELF-PORTRAIT)</u>, 1982-85.
Oil on canvas.
1.98 x 3.96 metres,
(6.5 x 13 feet).

Detail.

KNUDSEN

Christian Knudsen's paintings are concerned explicitly with giving form to the tension between the rational and the intuitive, building up shape, line and colour, layer on layer. The images of the paintings comprise the traces of their process. Sometimes an area painted white or yellow becomes the surface on which geometric shapes are drawn. Sometimes an area of colour instead of completely filling the surface, fades to an unfinished edge, revealing a grid drawn in pencil beneath it.

Like Charles Gagnon (see p. 40), an artist whom he greatly respects, Knudsen has long used photography in parallel to his painting. In some early pictures he exposed photographic images directly onto emulsion he had spread on the canvas. More often, however, his use of photography plays a conceptual role in the development of his paintings – photography standing 'for him between the openness of direct, everyday experience and the autonomous abstract language by which his pictures are made.'*

Knudsen's most recent work has shown a more painterly approach, in which he uses colour not only to define surface but to gain an elusive, expressive character. PHOENIX moves boldly in this direction.

The broad planes of colour found in his earlier paintings remain – a very pale field of yellow adjacent to one of dark umber over red underpainting, produces a primary tension between coolness and warmth. Cutting through these, disturbing their control of the space, is a swirling, irregular form in cadmium red. The reference is to the Phoenix, the mythical bird of regeneration, dynamically reborn in the division between light and darkness.

David Burnett, CHRISTIAN KNUDSEN. Saskatoon: Mendel Art Gallery, 1984. p. 7.

b. Vorup, Denmark: 1945. Moved to Canada, 1957.
BFA, Sir George Williams University, Montréal, Québec, 1970.
Lives in Montréal, Québec.

Painting installed February, 1988.
Cinéma Pointe-Claire, Montréal (Pointe-Claire), Québec.

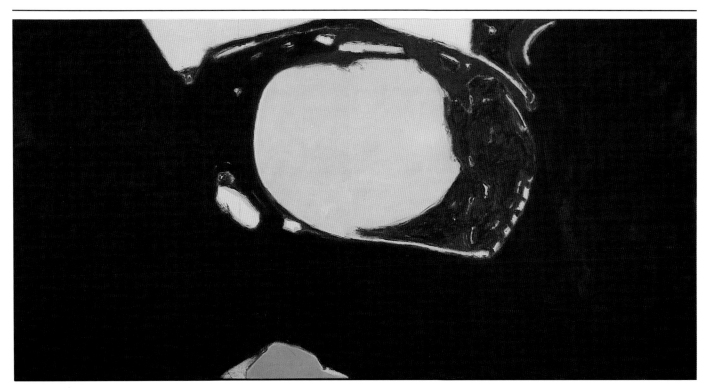

34. <u>PHOENIX</u>, 1987-88.
Acrylic on canvas.
1.83 x 3.66 metres,
(6 x 12 feet).

MARSHALL

One of the characteristics more notable in twentieth-century art than earlier periods has been the number of artist 'groups.' Such groups, however, range widely in structure and purpose. Painters Eleven in Toronto, for example, comprised artists of widely differing styles and interests. As a group they were able to find opportunities to exhibit their work that were unavailable to them as individuals. On the other hand, the Group of Seven and the Montreal group Les Automatistes, were formed to pursue more didactic goals.

In 1985 an exhibition entitled YOUNG ROMANTICS was held at the Vancouver Art Gallery.

The exhibition brought together eight young Vancouver painters. They do not form a group in the narrower sense. Their interest in recent European painting, their turn away from the tradition of landscape painting that has dominated painting in British Columbia, and the tough vitality of their work are common characteristics. The exhibition brought to national attention the work of a number of exciting and vibrant painters and Vicky Marshall, one of the 'Young Romantics,' has received a great deal of attention over the past four or five years.

Marshall's most recent paintings are of fruit, vegetables and flowers, richly painted in heavy impasto with colour that seems to glow from the inside. The Station Square Five Cinemas commission offered her the opportunity to extend these subjects. The theme for SCAVENGERS AND SUNFLOWERS was suggested when she came across a garbage dump near her studio located in the interior of British Columbia. She was struck not only by the irony of such a place in the wilderness but also by the way in which giant sunflowers were growing among the debris. The flowers not only contrast with the man-made ugliness but appear determined to heal the wound that has been made in their environment.

b. Sheffield, England: 1952. Moved to Canada, 1966.
Graduated from the Emily Carr College of Art, Vancouver, 1979.
Lives in Vancouver, British Columbia.

Painting installed December 1988.
Station Square Five Cinemas, Vancouver (Burnaby), British Columbia.

35. <u>SCAVENGERS AND SUNFLOWERS</u>, 1988.
Oil on canvas.
2.13 x 3.05 metres,
(7 x 10 feet).

MILL

In the mid-1950s, in reaction to the Automatiste movement, avant-garde painting in Montréal turned towards rigorous, geometric abstraction. This direction held the substantial role in advanced art in Montréal into the 1970s. By the mid 1970s, however, a broader range of issues concerned younger artists; their desire for expression was manifested in the exhibition of young Montréal artists entitled QUEBEC 75.

In the early 1970s, Richard Mill was making black and white paintings that were formally geometric and severely reductive. Their hard edged shapes and smooth surfaces all but eliminated the sense of the artist's manual activity.

In the later 1970s, the severe, exclusive character of these works gave way to others in which Mill seemed to question the earlier premises of his painting. He made one-colour paintings with broad, loose brush strokes, asserting their hand-made character. Subsequently, although still working in black and white and with simple geometric forms, his paintings became looser until the coolness of their geometry seemed in conflict with the activity of painting itself.

The 1980s has seen Mill broadening the formal structure of his work, and developing contrasts of strong painterly textures in a wide range of colours.

LUMIERE gave Mill the opportunity to develop a large scale work with a multitude of elements. The painting comprises several sections, a construction of painted elements and wooden forms in a broad and lively range of colours and textures. The title is a *double entendre:* LUMIERE refers not only to light – the essential factor in both painting and film – but also to Auguste and Louis Jean Lumière, brothers from Besançon, France, who in 1895 invented the CINEMATOGRAPHE, a combination of motion picture camera, printer and projector.

b. Québec City, Québec: 1949.
Studied at L'Ecole des Beaux-Arts de Québec, 1968-70;
Baccalauréat, Université Laval, Québec, 1971.
Lives in Québec City, Québec.
Painting installed October, 1986.
Cinémas Place Charest, Québec City, Québec.

36. <u>LUMIERE</u>, 1986.
Oil and acrylic on canvas and wood.
Irregular; 3.05 x 4.88 metres,
(10 x 16 feet).

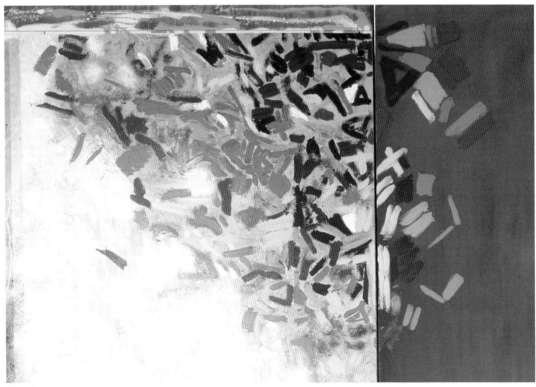

Detail.

MOPPETT

Ron Moppett once wrote about how he believes that artists deal in generalities; that any approach to representation must leave open possibilities for reading a work of art: 'I cultivate ambiguity and worry about contrivance.'* His work has always been characterized by the play of everyday objects and references in the world of the picture. This play of differences – and often surprising similarities – is created within the new reality, that of the painting.

SCREEN comprises five panels, each with its own image, structure, and manner of presentation. Common to the four lower panels are the forms of sticks and tree roots described in silhouette. The two panels on the left are schematic landscapes contrasting 'night' and 'day.' The fourth panel combines the two, setting the schematized colours of dawn against a starry night sky. The third panel, sets the same silhouette forms into a grid, as if to classify them: specimens in a museum, perhaps, or a system of signs. The violin and oar are artifacts made from the same material as the twigs and roots, suggesting another level of transformation and association. The longer we look at the silhouetted shapes, the more they lose their initial identities and suggest new possibilities for interpretation. The figures at the bottom of the right hand panel may be a photographer, a painter or a surveyor, all observers and transformers of the natural world. Above these images, in the fifth panel, hovers a teddy bear-cum-angel, a witty combination of a simple, comforting toy and an image of our hopes and fears beyond the everyday world. The whole is, Moppett says, 'as ordinary and as magical as a dream.'

*CURNOE/EWEN/FALK/MOPPETT
Regina: The Norman Mackenzie
Art Gallery. 1982. p.58.

*b. Woking, England: 1945.
Moved to Canada, 1957.
Graduated from the Alberta
College of Art, Calgary, 1967.
Lives in Calgary, Alberta.*

*Painting installed August 1988.
Northland Village Cinemas,
Calgary, Alberta.*

37. <u>SCREEN</u>, 1988.
Acrylic and mixed media on canvas.
Irregular; 3.66 x 7.01 metres,
(12 x 23 feet).

DE NIVERVILLE

As a young child, Louis de Niverville began to draw a world of fantasy. It provided an escape from the isolation and restrictions of an extended hospital stay. As a teenager and young adult he continued to draw, although he never had any formal art instruction. In 1957, he moved to Toronto and took some of his drawings to MACLEAN'S magazine where he was immediately assigned freelance illustration work. Subsequently, he was hired by the Canadian Broadcasting Corporation (CBC) as a designer where he remained for six years. He left the CBC after winning a commission for paintings for the Toronto International Airport. They are now located in the International Departures Lounge of Terminal 2. Other commissions followed and gallery exhibitions of his work in Toronto and elsewhere gained very positive receptions. There have been many changes in de Niverville's work during the thirty years of his professional career. But nothing has been lost of the magic and fantasy worlds of childhood experiences, worlds filled with wit and humour and, sometimes, the darkness and terror of nightmares.

THE MAPLE TREE is both ironic and playful. The image reaches up to twenty-five feet and spreads sixteen feet, a scale equal to that of a real tree. Yet the jig-saw form in which de Niverville presents his tree suggests that we approach it as if our world had undergone an 'Alice in Wonderland' change of scale. Fantasy and reality, like art and its images, relate and communicate through a continuous exchange of values.

b. Andover, England: 1933.
Moved to Canada, 1933.
Lives in Vancouver, British Columbia.

Painting installed December 1987.
Sherway Cinemas,
Toronto (Etobicoke), Ontario.

38. <u>THE MAPLE TREE</u>, 1987.
Acrylic on wood,
4.88 x 6.71 metres,
(16 x 22 feet).

NOESTHEDEN

He began his career as a print-maker, but for the past ten years John Noestheden has concentrated on sculpture and large-scale drawings. His early sculptures were austere, totemic images. Subsequently, he made wall-mounted pieces in bronze – linear structures of arcs and zig-zags, musical in their titles and rhythms. Unlike the formal elegance and crafted precision of the sculptures, Noestheden's drawings were gestural, open-ended, and layered with the process of ideas forming.

Five years ago Noestheden moved from Toronto north to a small rural community. The effect on his sculpture was immediate and substantial. His range of materials broadened; along with the bronze elements he fashioned, there then appeared natural objects he found close to hand, such as field stones and weathered tree branches, as well as pieces of discarded manufactured steel objects.

His mixed-media wall sculptures were small, but gradually the works spread over larger areas, confidently engaging the space. GLENELG CONCERTO is one of his most ambitious sculptures, both in scale and range of materials: bronze in various finishes, wood, field stones and granite slabs. In an area some ten feet high and forty-two feet long he forms a sculptural landscape, a composite of the natural and the man-made. With this work he has brought the openness and spontaneity of his drawings into his sculpture.

b. Amsterdam, The Netherlands: 1945.
Moved to Canada, 1952.
BFA, University of Windsor, Ontario, 1972;
MFA, Tulane University, New Orleans, 1975.
Lives in Priceville, Ontario.

Sculpture installed June 1988.
Spectrum Cinemas, Houston, Texas.

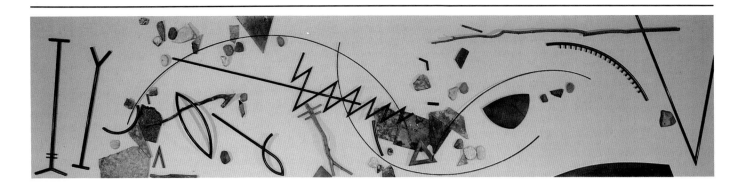

39. <u>GLENELG CONCERTO</u>,
1988. *Mixed media relief.*
Irregular; 2.74 x 12.80 metres,
(9 x 42 feet).

Detail.

OVERFIELD

Richard Overfield said recently, "Painters have a shared nervous system with poets. They should put more pressure on ideas, like writers. I want my paintings to nudge up against other disciplines, but not in a competitive way".*

His new paintings, which follow his earlier work in being based on grids, are presented like pages from a manuscript – abstracted visual images are repeated line by line, column by column. In the borders around the grid, texts are written in gold lettering. These images seem like inversions of medieval illuminated manuscripts in which the text was bordered by images of figures, animals and foliage, often enhanced with gold leaf.

HOW MANY SOLITUDES? is a painting Overfield has called a 'definition of transition'. It concerns the way languages are not only structures of communication, but carry within them broad cultural meaning – communal identity, national characteristics and political implications of conflict between dominant and minority societies. The painting is divided into three sections, predominantly black and white. The outer, black panels contain texts in English on the left, and French on the right – references to the two official languages of Canada. The white of the central panel is modified with soft touches of black and red. The red borders contain texts in other languages – Chinook, a trading language that combined English, French and native languages once used in the north west United States and British Columbia, and Inuit and Dene languages – but these have become illegible, concealed under layers of paint. The inflammatory red strips, containing the suppressed languages, are squeezed between the dominant extremes of black and white.

*In Ted Lindberg
RICHARD OVERFIELD.
New York and Toronto:
Stephen Rosenberg Gallery
and Galerie Dresdnere, 1988.*

b. Louisville, Kentucky: 1943. Moved to Canada 1978.
BA, Arizona State University, Tempe, Arizona, 1970;
Graduate studies at the University of Washington,
Seattle, Washington, 1972.
Lives in Vancouver, British Columbia.

Painting installed February 1988.
Genito Forest Cinemas, Richmond (Midlothian), Virginia.

40. <u>HOW MANY SOLITUDES?</u>, 1988.
Oil on canvas.
1.83 x 4.95 metres,
(6 x 16.25 feet).

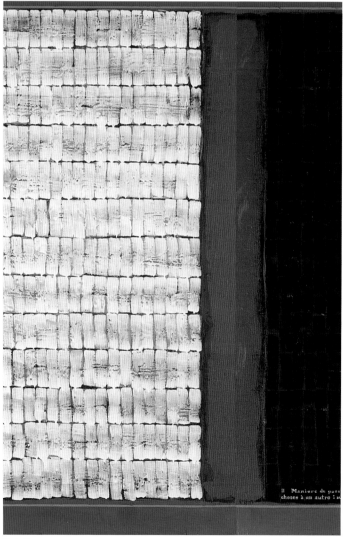

Detail.

RAYNER

At the core of Toronto's avant-garde of the mid and later 1950s were the artists of the 'Isaacs group,' so called because of their association with Av Isaacs, who opened the Greenwich Gallery in 1955 (renamed the Isaacs Gallery four years later). Among these artists were Dennis Burton, Graham Coughtry, Richard Gorman, Robert Markle, John Meredith, Michael Snow, Joyce Wieland (see p. 110), and Gordon Rayner.

Rayner trained as a commercial artist, first with his father and then with Jack Bush's commercial art company Wookey, Bush and Winter. Unlike many of the 'Isaacs Group,' who have emphasized figurative images, Rayner has taken landscape as the basis of much of his work. In addition, the exotic patterns and colours of artifacts seen on his travels have also been a major influence and his paintings, collages and constructions are characterized by richly coloured and exuberantly painted surfaces and witty invention.

All of these features are present in Rayner's thirty-five foot, mixed-media work at the Canada Square Cinemas. The structure comprises three quite distinct sections: the centre and right sections are two linked fans, their shape echoing an earlier series of paintings; the left section is a painted wood construction, like the vanes of a fan gone awry. The fans suggest the panoramic sweep of a movie camera while providing the overall rhythm of the work. The outside sections are linked by neon forms in pink and yellow, which play on the traditional use of neon in movie-house architecture. Rayner wittily describes the positioning of his work: the neon words 'Move' and 'Ease' describe the duality of the movie-going experience as both dynamic participation and a form of relaxation.

b. Toronto, Ontario: 1935.
Lives in Toronto, Ontario.

Painting installed December 1985.
Canada Square Cinemas,
Toronto, Ontario.

41. <u>MOVE-EASE</u>, 1985.
Mixed media.
Irregular; 4.57 x 10.67 metres,
(15 x 35 feet).

Detail.

RICHARDS

There is a mystery in all Phil Richards' works, a tension between the directness with which the surfaces are painted and the juxtapositions of figures and objects. Sometimes he will link aspects of the contemporary world with what remains of the past. Sometimes he integrates artifacts of other cultures in a modern western setting. Still other paintings concentrate on the play of children in imitation of and in contrast to the adult world, setting innocence and darker forces side by side. Using a striking realist technique, he unites the simple and the complex with wit and irony in ways that engage and disturb the appearance of the everyday world.

The commission at the Woodbine Centre gave Richards a special opportunity to explore the layers of realism and illusion inherent in movie mak-

ing. His painting is both an extension and an alternative to the lobby of the theatre. In black and white, he refers to past films – CITIZEN KANE and STAR WARS – and past stars – Fred Astaire, Ginger Rogers and James Stewart. He then brings these to life, or at least to the life of the painting, through portraits of his friends, who appear to take roles in movies. In the foreground he adds yet another level of reality, that of the movie-goer, through portraits of himself and his three sons. To cap off this complex layering of references to past and present, to the illusion of film and the reality of watching films, he contrasts 'his' theatre lobby, in the style of movie houses of the 1940s, with the architecture of the theatre lobby of the Woodbine Centre.

b. Toronto, Ontario: 1951.
Graduated from the Ontario
College of Art, Toronto 1973.
Lives in Toronto, Ontario.

Painting installed August 1985.
Woodbine Centre Cinemas,
Toronto (Etobicoke), Ontario.

42. <u>ONCE UPON A TIME</u>, 1985.
Acrylic on wood.
Irregular; 3.05 x 6.40 metres,
(10 x 21 feet).

Detail.

ROBERT

When we use the term 'the language of painting,' or describe how we are 'reading a painting,' we are admitting ourselves into a complex of illusions. They are charged terms, no matter whether we recognize the endless entanglements that arise between the forms of a language and the meanings we assume they hold, or accept the deception of a neutral exchange in meaning between visual and written forms.

In her drawings and paintings of the 1970s, Louise Robert's work stretched the tension between written and visual languages. Sometimes she would scribble words on the surfaces of her pictures, at other times she would structure her paintings like lines of print on a page, using only the loops and scrawls of graphic forms. Both types of work focus on the issue of meaningful communication: when and how are graphic forms transformed? At what point do written forms disappear, when do graphic forms signal letters and words?

In her paintings of the past ten years, Robert has approached the issue from another direction. She has been making strongly coloured and richly textured abstract paintings, often irregular in shape and comprised of overlapping layers of canvas. She does not attach the canvases to stretchers, but simply pins them to the wall; sometimes she allows them to curl over the floor. She writes phrases or sentences on the canvases, roughly, like graffiti. Robert creates tension through the ironic and ambiguous presentation of the works and the dissonance in the painted surfaces and the phrases scrawled on them. In OÙ EST LE YUCATAN? we must deal with an image and the enigmatic sentence written across it. However, we must also account for the painted wood shapes: they seem to fly off the painting, yet have counterparts within the painting. Just as we cast words into the air, so the elements of painting can be seemingly cast off, sounds and forms to be heard and seen, waiting to be reconstituted into logical linguistic forms.

b. Montréal, Québec: 1941.
Lives in Laval, Québec.

Painting installed September 1986.
Cinémas Carrefour Laval,
Montréal (Laval), Québec.

43. *Installation of*
OÙ EST LE YUCATAN?
in the lobby of
Cinémas Carrefour Laval.

Detail.

44. <u>OU EST LE YUCATAN?</u>, 1986.
Acrylic on canvas;
painted wood elements.
1.83 x 4.57 metres,
(6 x 15 feet) canvas.

ROGERS

Immediately after completing his studies, Otto Rogers joined the faculty of the University of Saskatchewan in Saskatoon, becoming Head of the Art Department in 1973. In 1988 he moved to Haifa to serve at the Baha'i Faith Centre.

Rogers' first introduction to art came from the landscape painter Wynona Mulcaster, but his feeling for landscape – the special character of light, space and texture of the prairie landscape – was founded during his childhood spent on a farm. His painting has always responded to both the physical and spiritual experience of landscape, without being *about* landscape in a descriptive sense. Formally, his work is abstract, the space of the paintings developed by broad divisions of the surface, overlapping planes, and contrasts of colour and texture. He has spoken of art as being a set of relationships 'the object of which is unity' but where 'to experience a sense of totality, a capacity to make use of variety must be developed.'*
That unity he has come to know through his religious faith, and has recognized its manifestation in the landscape.

For most of his paintings, Rogers has used formats that are close to square. In CELE-BRATION, however, he chose to work on a single, very broad canvas. He divided it into two horizontal planes, enclosed at each end by vertical elements, and articulated the depicted space with a series of dark silhouette forms. He has spoken of this painting as having a quality of 'moving elements in a time frame.' The diverse elements disposed across the pictorial space parallel the incidents of action in time as in a film.

*OTTO ROGERS: A SURVEY 1973-1982. Saskatoon: Mendel Art Gallery, 1982. pp. 29, 32.

b. Kerrobert, Saskatchewan: 1935.
BSc, Art Ed., 1959;
MSc, Fine Art, University of Wisconsin, Milwaukee, 1960
Lives in Haifa, Israel.

Painting installed April 1988.
Pacific Cinemas,
Saskatoon, Saskatchewan.

45. <u>CELEBRATION</u>, 1987-88.
Acrylic on canvas.
1.52 x 5.49 metres,
(5 x 18 feet).

Detail.

RONALD

In 1953, William Ronald, Harold Town, Jack Bush, Jock MacDonald, and seven other artists from Toronto and nearby cities formed PAINTERS ELEVEN. Throughout the 1950s, the group aggressively led the modernist art scene in Toronto. Many members of the group found an immediate source of pictorial interest and influence in the Abstract Expressionist movement in New York. Ronald, in particular, felt strongly drawn by its energy and opportunity, and moved to New York in 1954. During the eleven years he lived in the United States, he enjoyed considerable success with his forthright, gestural paintings shown in a number of exhibitions at the Samuel Kootz Gallery.

After he returned to Canada in 1965, Ronald earned a reputation as a notorious host of radio and television programs. For a few years he did little painting, until he received a mural commission for the National Arts Centre in Ottawa in 1969 which he dedicated as HOMAGE TO ROBERT KENNEDY. In recent years, his penchant for taking bold and often controversial stands, led him to paint THE PRIME MINISTERS OF CANADA, a series of subjective and expressionistic interpretations of Canada's leaders.

Ronald's work has always been hard-hitting, high-keyed and gestural: this is as true of SPENCER TRACY SINGS THE BLUES of 1987 as it is of his paintings of the late 1950s.

b. Stratford, Ontario: 1926.
Graduated from the Ontario College of Art, Toronto, 1951.
Lives in Montréal, Québec.

Painting installed August 1988.
Fantasy Cinemas,
New York (Rockville Centre), New York.

46. <u>SPENCER TRACY SINGS THE BLUES</u>, 1987.
Acrylic on canvas.
1.83 x 2.74 metres,
(6 x 9 feet).

SCHERMAN

Tony Scherman returned to Toronto in 1978 after having lived in England for many years. During the early 1980s his paintings concentrated on images of everyday objects isolated in undefined spaces. The clarity in description of the objects was countered by the richly textured painted surfaces, as if the objects were being absorbed into the space. The objects imply a human presence but, in its absence, stand only as emblems.

In recent years the central subject of Scherman's art has been food. Against the isolation that characterized his earlier work, his paintings now comprise multiple layers of imagery that respond to the rich veins of metaphor in his subject matter. In its gathering, preparation, presenta-tion and consumption, food is both natural and cultural. It is a necessity that is the core of a social history – manners and behaviour, attraction and revulsion, indulgence and taboos, national and class distinctions, intimate and ceremonial social interac-tion – can all be told in terms of food.

Scherman creates a multi-dimensional space. Images of food and of spectral or frag-mented figures seem to pass through the space as if several moments in time are over-lapped. In THE COMFORT OF FOOD this complexity of illu-sion is heightened by the way a sequence of disjointed events is spread across three panels. A table fills the fore-ground, gradually angling back into depth. On the left, the girl eating an ice-cream cone stands, and the dog lies on the table. In the centre, food – as in a traditional still-life painting – stands on it, attended by only the ghostly presence of a figure. On the right, the colour of the table changes from blue to red and a person, attended by a ser-vant, crudely scoops food from a bowl.

Scherman uses the ancient but now rare technique of wax encaustic. Pigments are combined with melted wax and applied hot to the sur-face. Then, in a process called 'blending-in,' the hardened surface is heated and the soft-ened wax is reworked with a knife and other tools to blend the colours and give texture to the surface.

b. Toronto, Ontario: 1950.
Studied at the Royal College
of Art, London, England.
Lives in Toronto, Ontario.

Painting installed December 1987.
Oakbrook Cinemas 1-3,
Chicago (Oak Brook), Illinois.

47. <u>THE COMFORT OF FOOD</u>, 1987.
Encaustic on canvas.
Three parts; 1.52 x 5.18 metres,
(5 x 17 feet).

Detail.

ROBERT SCOTT
WHITEMUD CROSSING SIX CINEMAS
EDMONTON, ALBERTA

SCOTT

Since the 1940s, when Jackson Pollock made his pictures by dripping and splattering paint on canvas, one aspect of modern painting has been concerned with the relationship between the process of painting and the development of the image. In particular, there has been a great deal of exploration in the methods of relating the image of the painting to the dynamics of its production. This approach balances on the edge between retaining complete control over working procedures and accepting chance or accident, neither forcing the former nor seeking to conceal the latter.

Some ten years ago, Robert Scott began to make his paintings by spraying layers of colour on his canvases and then raking his fingers through the paint. The overall formal appearance of the paintings developed through the pattern of grooves within the paint. This method also created the surface colour of the work as his raking disturbed and mixed the colour layers. In his most recent paintings, however, he has moved away from 'raking,' and has developed two contrasting approaches to the surfaces. One method builds the surfaces in high relief, the

paint swept up like wave crests on the point of turning. He generally uses one dominant colour, its effective range increased by the light breaking on the uneven paint surface. The second approach, found in the commissioned works CINITSUA and CINESU-BOBUS, involves spraying and splattering the paint. Relatively thin layers of colours play against one another in contrasting hues and graphic structures.

b. Melfort, Saskatchewan: 1941.
Graduated from the Alberta College of Art, Calgary, 1969.
MVA, University of Alberta, Edmonton, 1976.
Lives in Edmonton, Alberta.

Paintings installed December 1987.
Whitemud Crossing Six Cinemas,
Edmonton, Alberta.

48. <u>CINITSUA</u>, 1987. *(left)*
Acrylic on canvas.
2.06 x 4.40 metres,
(6.75 x 14.45 feet).

49. <u>CINESUBOBUS</u>, 1987. *(below)*
Acrylic on canvas.
2.21 x 4.42 metres,
(7.25 x 14.5 feet).

SHADBOLT

As a painter, teacher and writer, Jack Shadbolt has dominated the west-coast art scene for forty years. After wartime service with the Canadian Army War Art Program, he returned to teaching at the Vancouver School of Art. He was Head of the Drawing and Painting Section for many years, until his retirement in 1966. Exhibitions of his work have been held around the world and he has undertaken major com-missions in Canada for both public and corporate sites.

His paintings and drawings have been, in their subject matter and artistic process, celebrations of life observed in the rich flora and fauna of British Columbia and expressed in the art of the native cultures of the Northwest Coast. Shadbolt's work, always bold in its drawing and powerful in its colour, is a creative response in abstract pictorial terms to nature's forms and its inherent forces.

The Granville Cinemas work is massive and ambitious and its title TREE OF LIFE, is physically and dynamically appropriate. It is a painted, wooden relief construction, comprising hundreds of pieces of shaped plywood. Shadbolt has described its theme to be 'a transformation piece – art paraphrasing nature.'

TREE OF LIFE is a brilliant resolution of the complex restrictions dictated by the architecture of the site. The building prescrvcs two facades of the original street: on the southern end, the Palm Hotel, dating from 1894; to the north, Coronet Theatre, built in the 1930s. The only available site for a major work of art was in a narrow well, open to three floors, behind the facade. Shadbolt's work literally climbs up this well and spreads over the lobby balconies on the second and third floors. The construction is abstract in image, but here and there the forms of flowers and seed pods are apparent. These are 'symbolic suggestions,' he has said, 'of an underlying and irrepressible force of natural growth that would take over the available terrain for its own.'

b. Shoeburyness, England: 1909.
Moved to Canada, 1912.
Studied at the Art Students' League,
New York, 1928; Andre Lhote
School of Art, Paris, 1937;
Euston Road Art School,
London, 1937.
Lives in Vancouver, British Columbia.
Painting installed June 1987.
Granville Cinemas,
Vancouver, British Columbia.

50. *Installation of*
TREE OF LIFE seen from
(left) the third floor,
(right) the main floor lobbies
of the Granville Cinemas.

51. <u>TREE OF LIFE</u>, 1987.
Painted wood construction.
Irregular; 8.53 x 5.18 metres,
(28 x 17 feet).

Detail.

SHUEBROOK

Abstract modernist painting has a great range: from the unfettered gesture – accepting accidental marks and traces as necessary to gain expression of freedom – to geometric structures so precise and hermetic that their images conceal the process of their making. Ron Shuebrook's paintings stand mid-way between these extremes. They seek formal resolution but accept that there is no point of absolute equilibrium. They present the tension between the desire for order and the artist's self-critical questioning. Shuebrook's paintings are geometric in their forms and structures, yet invariably asymmetrical. They are rational in organization and yet gestural in the way they are made: arcing forms are described by the sweep of his arm, and the final image emerges only by a continuous reworking of the surfaces. He once described himself in a way that also expressed the tensions within his search for balance: 'I am, among other things, a maker, a fabricator of what Hannah Arendt has called thought-things.'*

SEQUENCE is a painting in three sections. Three hues and three graphic forms predominate: the curving arc, the straight edge, and the notched shape. Yet there is no repetition across the surface. Uniqueness is determined by shape, colour, or position. As we scan the picture we may see it as an abstracted schema of every possible combination. Or, we may recognize it as an attempt to reach an inviolable balance. The formal considerations of the painting are emphasized by being placed on a curved bulkhead. This stresses the visual dynamics as our eyes sweep the sequence.

*'Thinking and Making: Notes for the Duration' in RON SHUEBROOK. RECENT WORK/OEUVRES RECENTES.. Montréal: Concordia Art Gallery, 1986. p. 9.

b. Fort Monroe, Virginia: 1943.
Moved to Canada, 1972.
BS, 1965; MEd, 1969, Kutztown State College, Pennsylvania, 1969;
MFA, Kent State University, Ohio, 1972.
Lives in Guelph, Ontario.

Painting installed June 1988.
El Dorado Cinemas, Tucson, Arizona.

52. <u>SEQUENCE</u>, 1988.
Acrylic on canvas.
2.13 x 6.40 metres,
(7 x 21 feet).

Detail.

SLOGGETT

Paul Sloggett is a contemporary of those Toronto modernists such as Paul Hutner (see p. 52), who belong to what has been called the 'third generation of Toronto modernist painters' (see above p.16). Unlike many of his contemporaries, however, whose work involves figurative or landscape elements, Sloggett's paintings remain more rigorously abstract in structure and form. He does share with other contemporary modernists an artistic debt to Jack Bush. Sloggett's work of the 1970s drew on Bush's later work in its formal and contrasting textural elements. His approach is geometric, architectural. He often uses firmly delineated elements that appear to be in the process of formation; these are set against soft atmospheric grounds. He builds the compositions of contrasting planes of shape and texture, one layer opening on another.

ISHI'S DREAM, like some other recent Sloggett works, is a logical extension of his paintings in more conventional formats. Here he breaks that format, constructing a relief painting in which the formal elements are no longer defined within a rectangular canvas, but spin outwards from the circular heart of the construction. The title refers to another interest of Sloggett's; Ishi was an Indian of the Yaqui tribe of the South West who reintroduced archery as a modern sport.

b. Campbellford, Ontario: 1950.
Graduated from the Ontario
College of Art, Toronto, 1973.
Lives in Toronto, Ontario.

Painting installed June 1988.
Holladay Center Cinemas,
Salt Lake City, Utah.

53. <u>ISHI'S DREAM</u>, 1988.
Acrylic on canvas mounted on wood.
Irregular; 3.35 x 3.66 metres,
(11 x 12 feet).

SUTTON

In the mid-1970s Carol Sutton met the painters Kenneth Noland and Jack Bush and the art critic Clement Greenberg. She acknowledges the influence that the work of Noland and Bush has had on her and the guidance she has received from Greenberg. Her painting has been described as 'an art of enrichment rather than extremity'* – abstract painting, having by its history revealed the extremes of its methods, holds the potential for an infinite range with possibilities, as varied as the individual artists themselves.

Sutton's paintings have investigated a number of formal directions. There have been groups of paintings based on sweeping diagonals, groups based on swirling nebulae and on spirals. Through all of them, however, there are characteristic, recurring gestures and means of structuring colour – for example, the way she heightens colour effects by having bands of several hues following the

same vectors, and her use of a certain waving, scallop-like gesture in shaping forms.

In EYE OF THE OVAL, Sutton worked towards the particular conditions of the site – the strongly horizontal format and the fact that the painting, directly facing the main entrance of the cinema, would be seen both from a considerable distance and from close up. Sutton has described the painting as being about seeing. She said, 'This EYE OF THE OVAL is a Southern eye, sees green, sees clear, as if underwater in some tropical sea, sees languid dripping forms, sees nature with a backhand stroke, sees motion, sees emotion moving, sees sunlight, sees color, and finally looks back into and sees itself.'

*Walter Darby Bannard
CAROL SUTTON. WATER SPIRALS AND AQUA NEBULA.
Toronto: Gallery One, 1983.

b. Norfolk, Virginia: 1945.
Moved to Canada, 1970.
BFA, Richmond Professional Institute, Richmond, Virginia;
MFA, University of North Carolina.
Lives in Toronto, Ontario.

Painting installed May 1987.
Sand Lake Seven Cinemas,
Orlando, Florida.

54. <u>EYE OF THE OVAL</u>, 1987.
Acrylic on canvas.
2.29 x 5.49 metres,
(7.5 x 18 feet).

Detail.

TAMASAUSKAS

Otis Tamasauskas was commissioned to create an original, unique print for the Edina Cinemas – to date, the only print work that has been commissioned for the Art Program. Very special printing skills are required to make prints large enough for a lobby space and to lay down colour that has the richness and density to be successful both when viewed from a distance and under close scrutiny. In addition to his own work, Tamasauskas has also collaborated with painters and sculptors to produce prints of their images. Since 1980 he has also taught lithography and etching at Queen's University, Kingston.

For THE RUNNING FOREST SERIES Tamasauskas used a woodcut technique, progressively carving and printing each colour using sheets of plywood. The prints are carried on handmade paper made to the artist's specifications by a Montréal papermaker.

The density and richness of the prints reflect the narrative images of the two prints which are best described by the artist's extended title for the work: 'When the rain stopped, the watchers of the forest came out, smiled and told stories of a river that shimmered and sparkled with silver and golden trout. Soon it started to rain again, smiles disappeared, tears ran down their eyes – they returned to the forest forever.'

b. Terschenreuth, Germany: 1947.
BFA, University of Windsor, 1974.
Lives in Priceville, Ontario.

Prints installed December 1988.
Edina Cinemas,
Minneapolis (Edina), Minnesota.

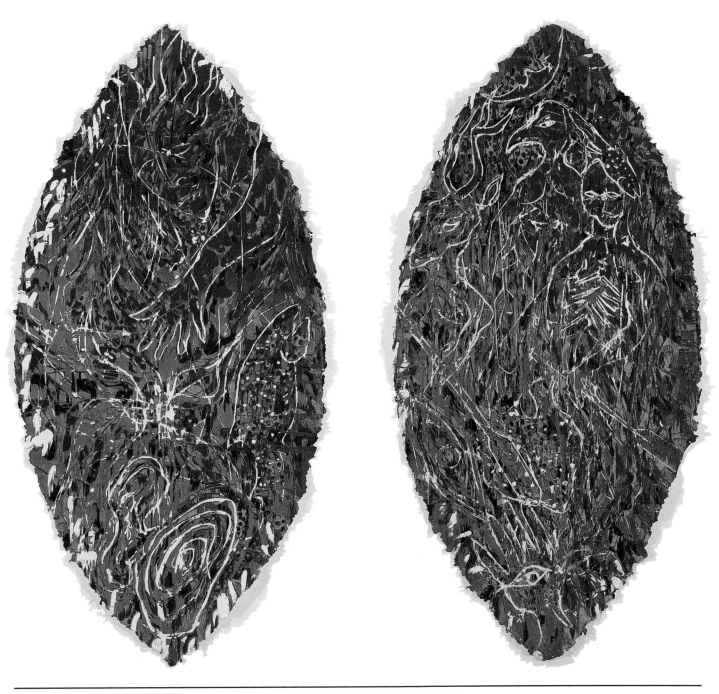

55. THE RUNNING FOREST SERIES, 1988.
Unique woodcut prints on handmade paper.
Two parts; 1.83 x .91 metres, (6 x 3 feet) each,
1.93 x 2.18 metres (6.33 x 7.17 feet) overall.

THAUBERGER

During the early 1970s, an interest in folk art and the influence of the American sculptor David Gilhooley led a number of Regina artists – including Joe Fafard, Russell Yuristy and David Thauberger – to make figurative sculpture in ceramic. Thauberger subsequently turned to painting.

The vernacular architecture of the city, both private homes and public buildings, became his main subject. He painted them like portraits, with all the pride and awkwardness of people in a family photograph album. Just as these images become emblems of the every-day, picture postcards capture the experience of the wider world. Thauberger has used postcards as the basis for a number of paintings, including for example, Niagara Falls and the geyser Old Faithful in Yellowstone National Park. His technique encapsulates the transformation of monuments of natural beauty into kitsch mementos.

Recently, Thauberger has become fascinated by the architecture and settings of the 1939 New York World's Fair, particularly their projection in souvenir postcards. Two of such postcards became the subjects Thauberger chose for his Cloverleaf Cinemas paintings. They provide an imaginative link between the contemporary film theatre and the futuristic presentation of communications and technology during the first great age of movie entertainment.

b. Holdfast, Saskatchewan: 1948. BFA, University of Saskatchewan, Regina, 1971; MA, California State University, Sacramento, 1972; MFA, University of Montana, Missoula, 1973. Lives in Regina, Saskatchewan.

Paintings installed April 1988. Cloverleaf Cinemas, Richmond, Virginia.

56. <u>COMMUNICATIONS AND
TECHNOLOGY A</u>, 1987. *(left)*
Acrylic and glitter on canvas.
2.13 x 3.05 metres,
(7 x 10 feet).

57. <u>COMMUNICATIONS AND
TECHNOLOGY B</u>, 1987. *(below)*
Acrylic and glitter on canvas.
2.13 x 3.05 metres,
(7 x 10 feet).

TOWN

The Universal City Cinemas is one of the world's largest cinema complexes, with eighteen screens and six thousand seats under one roof. The vast main lobby demanded works that would complement its scale, and yet provide a focus for the individual spectator.

The immediate choice for this commission was Harold Town, an artist of prodigious inventiveness and pictorial versatility. Town's response to the challenge was two massive paintings, each ten by eighteen feet, to flank the lobby. The paintings are visually dynamic and complex in incident and texture; yet, because of their vibrant colour and graphic clarity, they maintain their integrity from all the viewing angles. The formal character of STAGES I and STAGES II originated in a series of small-scale paintings, also called STAGES, that Town began in late 1986. These works were made by drawing and painting pieces of mattboard of diminishing size which were then stacked and glued together; each level was treated in a distinct graphic, textural, and colouristic manner. In STAGES I and STAGES II Town expanded this concept to monumental scale, a process that necessitated devising a complex support structure. Each of the paintings comprises seven interlocking wood frames, over each of which canvas is stretched.

Town's working method was established in the 1950s when he was a member of the Toronto group Painters Eleven (see p. 84). It involves the development of a particular idea through a series which may comprise from twenty works, to many hundreds. Each of these series – paintings or drawings, collages or prints, ranging from pure abstraction to precise figurative representation – is distinct in style, content, and technique. Like every Town series, the STAGES are unique yet, in their energy, inventiveness, and boldness, unmistakably Town.

b. Toronto, Ontario: 1924.
Graduated from the Ontario College of Art, Toronto, 1944.
Lives in Toronto, Ontario.

Paintings and drawings installed July 1987.
Universal City Cinemas, Los Angeles (Universal City), California.

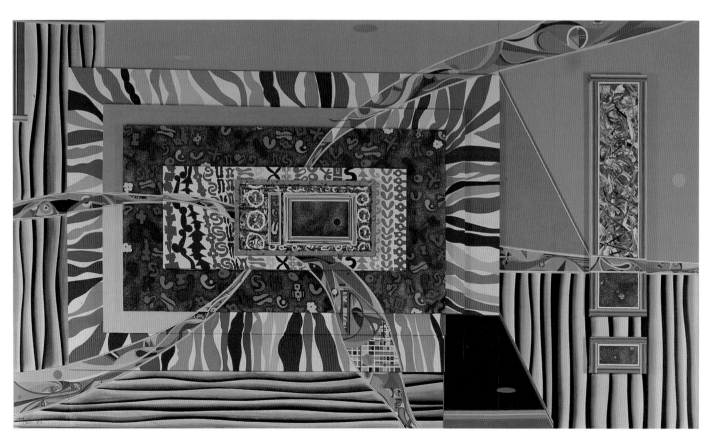

58. <u>STAGES I</u>, 1987. *(left)*
Oil and acrylic on canvas;
Relief construction.
3.05 x 5.49 metres,
(10 x 18 feet).

59. <u>STAGES II</u>, 1987. *(below)*
Oil and acrylic on canvas;
Relief construction.
3.05 x 5.49 metres,
(10 x 18 feet).

THE FAMOUS

The Universal City Cinemas location, adjacent to Universal Studio Tours, called for special recognition in the Art Program. On the first floor there are six seating niches. On the walls of each niche a pair of pencil drawings by Harold Town is installed. These twelve drawings were commissioned specifically for this site, but they relate to another of Town's series, one that he began in 1984. It was based on photographs of famous people, politicians, writers, musicians and film stars, and was called THE FAMOUS. Each of the drawings at Universal City Cinemas is based on a scene from a film produced by Universal Studios. They range from THE DEVIL'S PASSKEY (1919) and THE PHANTOM OF THE OPERA (1925) to BACK TO THE FUTURE (1986).

Unlike the vibrant, monumental STAGES paintings in the lobby, these subtle and fine FAMOUS drawings set a quiet, contemplative mood. Together the STAGES and THE FAMOUS exemplify Town's extraordinary range and versatility.

Detail.

60. ALL QUIET ON THE WESTERN FRONT 1930,
LOUIS WOLHEIM & LEW AYRES, 1987. *(right)*
Pencil on NpH rag board.
45.72 x 38.10 centimetres,
(18 x 15 inches).

VAN DYCK

Yolanda Van Dyck was studying microbiology at the University of Calgary when she decided to pursue her long held interest in art. She then studied painting and printmaking in Edmonton, Banff, and St. Michael's, Newfoundland. She returned to Calgary, where she graduated from the Alberta College of Art. She has continued studying dance, video, anatomy and African art history. For two years, she was artist in residence at the Leighton Artists Colony in Banff.

It is usually tautological to describe an artist's work as being personal – except, of course, for those artists who choose to eliminate marks of personality from their work. To speak of Van Dyck's work as personal, however, is to describe how she has set herself apart from the general directions and styles of the time in order to express individual concerns in terms of their own particularity.

Some paintings and drawings reveal a raw edginess; others embody a lightness and delicacy of touch, as much calligraphic as painterly. THE SILVER SCREEN is of this latter sort. In it Van Dyck overlays two ideas: the silver screen as a ground over which images play, and a screen of flowers as if panned by a movie camera which captures and sets them in motion.

b. Glasgow, Scotland.
Moved to Canada, 1955.
Graduated from the Alberta
College of Art, Calgary, 1979.
Lives in Calgary, Alberta.

Painting installed December 1987.
London Town Square Cinemas,
Calgary, Alberta.

61. THE SILVER SCREEN, 1987.
Acrylic on canvas.
1.83 x 5.49 metres,
(6 x 18 feet).

Detail.

WEBB

In general terms, modernist art in Edmonton has tended to be dominated by abstract colour field painting – see, for example, Phil Darrah (p. 28), Doug Haynes (p. 50) and Robert Scott (p. 88) – and abstract welded steel sculpture. Calgary, in contrast, has long had a more diversified art scene – the work of John Hall (p. 46), Ron Moppett (p. 68) and Yolanda Van Dyck (p. 106), for example, represents some of that diversity. Ken Webb, a young Calgary painter, has established an individual direction with his dark, richly painted images based on architectural forms. Webb's paintings recall the classical architectural heritage – a heritage we know by archaeological discoveries, surviving buildings and their influence on later styles. The geometry of his art responds to the rational structure of that heritage, just as his dark, shadowy images reflect a past that we only dimly recognize as a source for our culture. Here and there in his paintings, areas of bright colour – touches of blue or red or gold – seem to suggest the presence of a more revealing light.

In many of Webb's paintings the elements are assembled in overlapping structures; they hold rigidly to the flatness of the surface while suggesting a mysterious, deep space. For his painting, COLLECTIVE REFLECTION, Webb has extended his approach to the depiction of space by making the elements in his picture – columns, vases and sections of architecture – as a series of separate panels. The space within the panels is thus combined with the space of the theatre architecture, uniting the real world and the virtual world of the painting.

b. Swalwell, Alberta: 1950.
Graduated from the Alberta College of Art, Calgary, 1976;
Studied at the Royal College of Art, London, England, 1977-78.
Lives in Calgary, Alberta.

Painting completed in 1988;
to be installed in 1989.

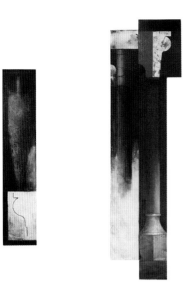
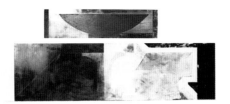

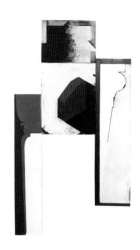

62. <u>COLLECTIVE REFLECTION</u>,
1988. *Acrylic, marble dust and
sand on masonite panels.
Ten panels; 2.74 x 8.53 metres,
(9 x 28 feet) overall.*

Detail.

WIELAND

As recently as six years ago it could still be said that Joyce Wieland had yet to gain broad recognition for her achievements in twenty-five years of making art and films. Recently, however, that oversight has been appreciably rectified by important exhibitions of her art and major screenings of her films in many parts of the world.

She first worked as a film animator, and made her first independent film in 1958. She showed her art first at the Greenwich Gallery in 1959, and was the only woman among the 'Isaacs Group' (see p. 76) of artists. Between 1964 and 1972 she lived in New York; her art and films, already radical in form and content, took on a more aggressive expression of nationalist and women's issues during this period. In 1971 she became the first woman to have a major retrospective exhibition at the National Gallery of Canada. (She centred the exhibition on the Canadian heroine Laura Secord.) Her advocacy of women's issues was demonstrated by her use of crafts traditionally undertaken by women, for example, her quilts TRUE PATRIOT LOVE and REASON OVER PASSION. It must be remembered that at the time, in the late 1960s, such artistic statements by women artists were uncommon.

In 1976 her film THE FAR SHORE, based on the life of the painter Tom Thomson, was released commercially. She returned to painting in the 1980s with a number of striking and provocative canvases. CELEBRATION was commissioned for the lobby of the Pantages Theatre. It is a joyous celebration of the history of film, reaching back to 1920, when the Pantages first opened, and, in imaginative terms, to the birth of the genre.

The Pantages Theatre has undergone many changes. In 1929 it was renamed the Imperial, and in 1973 became the Imperial Six when it was divided into six smaller cinemas. In 1986 Cineplex Odeon acquired half of the property, which opened as a single-screen cinema. After acquiring the remainder of the property in 1988 the Corporation undertook the restoration of the building, recreating the original Pantages for use as a legitimate theatre. Due to this recent change, the Joyce Wieland painting had to be removed and is now on extended loan to the Art Gallery of Hamilton.

*b. Toronto, Ontario: 1931.
Graduated from Central
Technical School, Toronto.
Lives in Toronto, Ontario.*

*Painting installed December 1987.
Pantages Theatre,
Toronto, Ontario.*

63. <u>CELEBRATION</u>, 1987.
Oil and canvas.
2.13 x 4.57 metres,
(7 x 15 feet).

Detail.

WOOD

Alan Wood was the first artist contracted to the Art Commission Program and his painting, THE MOVIES, was the first to be installed in a theatre. It remains one of the largest works in the Program – fourteen feet high at its centre point and thirty-six feet long. Working on a large scale, however, is nothing new for Wood. In 1983 he completed a temporary installation, RANCH which comprised fourteen large-scale painted constructions set onto a 320-acre site near Priddis, Alberta. The RANCH project expressed Wood's fascination with the western landscape and the structure of its settlements, and incorporated his boyhood memories of western movies.

The canvas and wood construction of RANCH is carried over into THE MOVIES, but here the combination of open framework and painted areas suggests the temporary structures of movie sets. Wood divided THE MOVIES into five 'scenes,' each representing in emblematic form a major genre in movie history. He described them as 'The Hollywood Musical,' 'Space Movies,' 'Westerns,' 'War Movies,' and 'Romance – the Screen Kiss.'

The asymmetrical shape of Wood's painting is a response to its location: it is set on the wall above the escalator. The work is adapted to the movement of viewers travelling up and down the escalator. The painting is also visible across the lobby at both the upper and lower levels. Wood has united these different viewpoints in a strong graphic and colouristic presentation, particularly noted in the contrast between the two-dimensionality of the painting's outline and the winding 'yellow brick road' that appears to carry the viewer into THE MOVIES.

b. Widnes, England: 1935.
Moved to Canada, 1974.
Studied at the Liverpool School of Art, 1954-59.
Lives in Vancouver, British Columbia.

Painting installed May 1985.
Oakridge Centre Cinemas,
Vancouver, British Columbia.

64. <u>THE MOVIES</u>, 1985.
Acrylic on canvas on wood.
Irregular; 4.27 x 10.97 metres,
(14 x 36 feet).

Detail.

ZELDIN

Gerald Zeldin's work ranges from small prints to large scale public commissions. Among the latter are painted murals at the Eaton Centre and Ontario Place in Toronto, and two porcelain enamel-on-steel murals for the Toronto Transit Commission, at its Eglinton West Station.

His recent paintings are playful and inventive. Objects from the adult world are transposed into toys, and people are turned into the stick figures of children's drawings. Zeldin often turns the rules of spatial and perspectival representation back on themselves and creates a world we recognize but cannot inhabit, much as adults recall the world of their childhood but can no longer live in it.

LIGHT BREEZE is an imaginative response to the role of the writer in cinema. The painting puts us in the place of a writer sitting at his desk, seeing a sequence from a story he has yet to write. In front of him is an urban setting in which stick-like figures, symbolizing, perhaps, character outlines, run around within it. Pencils lie on the table, ready for use. Across this scene sweeps the light from a movie projector, as if the writer were already able to visualize his part in the creative process transposed onto film.

b. Toronto, Ontario: 1943.
Graduated from the Ontario
College of Art, Toronto, 1965.
MFA, Claremont Graduate School,
Claremont, California, 1967.
Lives in Dundas, Ontario.
Painting installed December 1987.
Oakville Mews Five Cinemas,
Oakville, Ontario.

65. <u>LIGHT BREEZE</u>, 1987.
Acrylic on canvas.
2.74 x 6.71 metres,
(9 x 22 feet).

Detail.

CARLTON CINEMAS

The Carlton Cinemas were first opened by Cineplex Odeon in 1981. The complex developed as an 'art house' through the presentation of specialty and foreign films and is now one of North America's premiere art cinemas. The Carlton Cinemas were closed for renovation in the fall of 1987 and reopened in the Spring of 1988.

The specialized film offerings of the Carlton Cinemas created a unique opportunity for the Art Program. Instead of commissioning a single work, prints and drawings by eighteen leading artists were installed in the café and lobby areas. Like the films shown at the Carlton Cinemas, these works encompass a wide range of styles and techniques.

Six of the artists represented have been included elsewhere in the Program: Yves Gaucher, in Washington D.C. (see p. 42); Harold Klunder, in Chicago (see p. 60); Louis de Niverville, in Toronto (see p. 70); Gordon Rayner, in Toronto (see p. 76); Otis Tamasauskas, in Minneapolis (see p. 98); and David Thauberger, in Richmond, Virginia (see p. 100). There are also prints by realist artists, Alex Colville, Christopher Pratt, and Jeremy Smith, whose paintings are of a size and character that do not lend themselves to the large-scale work that characterizes most commissions in the Program.

Works by four artists who are best known as printmakers, Jan Winton, Ed Bartram, J.C. Heywood, and the late Don Phillips are displayed. Included also are prints by four major contemporary Canadian painters – Ronald Bloore, Graham Coughtry, Jean McEwen and Guido Molinari – whose works do not appear elsewhere in the Program. Finally, there is also a print by the late Jack Bush, whose example and influence is still strongly felt by many Canadian artists.

*Works on paper by eighteen artists installed April 1988.
Carlton Cinemas,
Toronto, Ontario.*

66. *(left to right)*
Don Phillips, <u>UNTITLED</u>, 1983. *Lithograph.*
Harold Klunder, <u>UNTITLED (PORTRAIT STUDY)</u>, 1981. *Mixed media.*
Ed Bartram, <u>PRECAMBRIAN RUNE #11</u>, 1987. *Etching.*

67. *(left to right)*
Otis Tamasauskas, <u>UNDER THE ARTEMESIA BRIDGE I SAW MANY MYSTERIES, I DECIDED TO STAY</u>, 1987. *Lithograph and screenprint.*
Graham Coughtry, <u>UNTITLED (ORANGE)</u>, 1979. *Lithograph.*

68. Gordon Rayner, <u>UNTITLED (VERTICAL)</u>, 1979. *Lithograph.*

69. *(below, left to right)*
Jean McEwen, <u>L'ETE</u>, 1973. *Lithograph.*
Yves Gaucher, <u>FENTE</u>, 1986-87. *Lithograph.*
Christopher Pratt, <u>SUMMER ON THE SOUTH EAST</u>, 1987. *Serigraph.*
Alex Colville, <u>GOLDEN DOG</u>, 1987. *Serigraph.*
Ronald Bloore, <u>UNTITLED</u>, 1986. *Ink Drawing.*

70.HAROLD TOWN.
Universal City Cinemas,
Los Angeles (Universal City),
California.

REVIVAL *of the* URBAN THEATRE

Twenty years ago there were many who bade farewell to urban life as we had known it. As urban centers were being abandoned, suburbs and suburban malls proliferated. Many assumed that the life of the 'Urban Theatre' – Teatro Mondi – was over.

In the early 70's Faneuil Hall Marketplace lay abandoned in the heart of Boston. The old city of Montreal was yet another dilapidated district, and property values in Manhattan and Chicago plummeted. The experts told us we were undergoing a major shift in behavior. With the advent of television, we were advised that people would retreat to their reclusive shells, and in the security and privacy of the home would come an end to the great urban meeting places.

As the exodus from the cities continued, the theatres and cinemas built earlier in the century were ravaged, others demolished, many subdivided into minimalist cubes, resembling windowless, faceless offices, dubbed the new cinema.

Television is here to stay, and undoubtedly, so is home video and the next generation of high fidelity–audio visual system. All notwithstanding, we are witnessing a renaissance, a rediscovery of the virtues and the qualities of urban life. Faneuil Hall, old Montreal, the Toronto Waterfront, and the downtown of each of these respective cities, are once again thriving enterprises. With this resurgence, so has the city as urban theatre, and the theatre and cinema as its significant ingredients, re-emerged.

The prolificacy of Cineplex Odeon cinemas across the continent must be seen and understood in that context. No longer is the drab lobby and minimalist box adequate. Going to the theatre must involve a sense of ceremony and celebration, entertainment in its fullest sense, for which the appropriate physical environment is required. Ornament and decoration are back, as are the exuberance and fascination with public places. A place of entertainment is also a place of meeting.

"Tear down the museum walls", said André Malraux in his well-known book LA MUSEE IMAGINAIRE, forecasting, anticipating the demise of the museum as an elitist institution. Since then the place of art in our public life has been radically transformed. The museums, once introvert ivory towers, have opened their doors and torn down their solid walls, exposing themselves to the public; replacing solemn pomposity with joyful seductiveness. More relevant, we now dream of the presence of visual art as engulfing and extending our lives everywhere. We think of great exhibitions on various subjects, whose galleries might be our subway cars and subway stations. When unleased space in Faneuil Hall Marketplace was turned over to the Boston Museum of Fine Arts, it became one of the highest in attendance. We now consider the lobbies of commercial buildings – indeed cinemas – to be legitimate extensions of the old museums.

Cineplex Odeon is a pioneer, creating a program which at once provides a setting for art in public places, while at the same time serving as a catalyst to encourage the activities and development of both well-known and yet-to-be-discovered artists. The cynics will say that this is undoubtedly a policy of good investment, and indeed it may be. It is with equal certainty, however, a program that encourages both the creation and appreciation of the visual arts. As the new agenda is established, striving to make the new cinema a memorable and exciting place, the artist has been called to contribute to that process.

For now, we enjoy the works in accordance with our tastes and inclinations, but it whets our appetite for more. One of the faults of contemporary architecture has been that it has created a schism, a separation, of the art of architecture and the visual arts. We are all too familiar with the office tower lobbies, restaurants and public buildings, whose architecture leaves us wanting and which the "1% for Art" program, or a private equivalent, seeks to repair by embellishment with sculpture or murals. The great experiences of architectural space in the past were not when art was placed in architecture, but when artist and architect collaborated, creating a harmony between the two works. Indeed, their best examples demonstrated that the sum total is much greater than the parts.

One hopes that this ambitious program of recreating the urban theatre will further evolve, creating the opportunity for significant architecture and art to be created as an integrated whole.

Moshe Safdie

71. LOUIS DE NIVERVILLE.
Sherway Cinemas,
Toronto (Etobicoke),
Ontario.

72. PETER ASPELL.
Marina MarketPlace Cinemas,
Los Angeles (Marina del Rey),
California.

73.WALTER BACHINSKI
Fairway Cinemas,
Kitchener, Ontario.

74.BRIAN BURNETT.
Palace Cinemas,
Windsor, Ontario.

75.DOUGLAS KIRTON.
RiverTree Court at Hawthorn,
Chicago (Vernon Hills),
Illinois.

76.WILL GORLITZ.
Fairview Cinemas,
Toronto (North York),
Ontario.

77.GORDON RAYNER.
*Canada Square Cinemas
Toronto, Ontario.*

78.DAVID BOLDUC.
*Madison Cinemas,
Toronto (North York),
Ontario.*

79. WILLIAM RONALD.
Fantasy Cinemas,
New York (Rockville Centre),
New York.

80. ULYSSE COMTOIS.
River Oaks Cinemas 1-6,
Chicago (Calumet City),
Illinois.

81.JOHN NOESTHEDEN
Spectrum Cinemas,
Houston, Texas.

82.TONY SCHERMAN.
Oakbrook Cinemas 1-3,
Chicago (Oak Brook),
Illinois.

83.JOSEPH DRAPELL.
Promenade Cinemas,
Toronto (Thornhill),
Ontario.

84.PAUL FOURNIER.
Centre Mall Theatres,
Hamilton, Ontario.

INDEX

End Papers:
Harold Town, <u>THE FAMOUS</u>
from Universal City Cinemas,

85. <u>TOUCH OF EVIL 1958,</u>
<u>ORSON WELLES JANET LEIGH,</u>
<u>AKIM TAMIROFF,</u> 1987.
Pencil on NpH rag board.
45.72 x 38.10 centimetres,
(18 x 15 inches).

86. <u>MY MAN GODFREY 1936,</u>
<u>WILLIAM POWELL & CAROLE LOMBARD,</u> 1987.
Pencil on NpH rag board.
45.72 x 38.10 centimetres,
(18 x 15 inches).

87. <u>THE DEVIL'S PASSKEY,</u>
<u>ERICH VON STROHEIM USA 1919;</u>
<u>MAE BUSCH MAUDE GEORGE,</u> 1987.
Pencil on NpH rag board.
45.72 x 38.10 centimetres,
(18 x 15 inches).

PHOTO CREDITS

Commissioned Works
Ellis Bartkiewicz: 25
Pierre Charrier: 43
Lauren Dale: 29
John Dean: 69
Don Hall: 18, 19
Zach Hauser: 49, 83
Robert Keziere: 13
Gerry Kitchen: 107
Eleanore Lazare: 51
Micheline Lévesque: 67
Louis Lussier: 27, 40, 41, 63, 80, 81
Trevor Mills: 37, 65, 113
Thomas Moore: endpapers, 15, 17, 23,
  31, 35, 39, 45, 47, 52, 53, 55, 57, 59,
  75, 77 (detail), 79, 87, 93, 95, 97, 99,
  100, 101, 104, 105, 111, 115
Larry Ostrom: 21, 61
Richard Siemans: 88, 89
Fiona Spalding-Smith: 71, 73, 77, 90,
  91, 102, 103, 116, 117
Henk Visser: 33
Ken Webb: 109

Installations
Christopher Casler: 11
Micheline Lévesque: 128
© Peter Mauss/ESTO: 8, 9, 124 (top)
Thomas Moore: 121, 126
Fiona Spalding-Smith: 118, 120, 122,
  124 (bottom), 125
Feature Four Limited: 123

Artists' Photos
Russell Bingham: 88
Catherine Carmichael: 60
Paul Chapnick: 16, 18, 20, 24, 36, 40,
  42, 48, 50, 56, 58, 76, 82, 84, 86, 90,
  94, 96, 110
John Dean: 106
Louis Lussier: 26
Tawny Maclachlan: 30
Ken McGinnis: 108
Trevor Mills: 64, 112
Thomas Moore: 14, 22, 44, 52, 70, 78,
  102, 114
Abbey Newman: 54
Jeff Nolte: 38
Jacques Payette: 80
Jurgen Vogt: 12
Toronto Sun, Canada Wide,
  S. Behal: 32

Cineplex Odeon, The First Ten Years
was originally published by Cineplex
Odeon Corporation, 1989.

Design
Scott Thornley, Cara-Lynn Rumack,
Thornley/Interchange Inc.

Art Production
Charlene Codner,
Thornley/Interchange Inc.

Typesetting
Cooper & Beatty.

Printed in Canada by
Arthurs-Jones Lithographing Ltd.

INDEX

End Papers:
Harold Town, <u>THE FAMOUS</u>
from Universal City Cinemas,

85. <u>TOUCH OF EVIL 1958</u>,
<u>ORSON WELLES JANET LEIGH</u>,
<u>AKIM TAMIROFF</u>, 1987.
Pencil on NpH rag board.
45.72 x 38.10 centimetres,
(18 x 15 inches).

86. <u>MY MAN GODFREY 1936</u>,
<u>WILLIAM POWELL & CAROLE LOMBARD</u>, 1987.
Pencil on NpH rag board.
45.72 x 38.10 centimetres,
(18 x 15 inches).

87. <u>THE DEVIL'S PASSKEY</u>,
<u>ERICH VON STROHEIM USA 1919</u>;
<u>MAE BUSCH MAUDE GEORGE</u>, 1987.
Pencil on NpH rag board.
45.72 x 38.10 centimetres,
(18 x 15 inches).

PHOTO CREDITS

Commissioned Works
Ellis Bartkiewicz: 25
Pierre Charrier: 43
Lauren Dale: 29
John Dean: 69
Don Hall: 18, 19
Zach Hauser: 49, 83
Robert Keziere: 13
Gerry Kitchen: 107
Eleanore Lazare: 51
Micheline Lévesque: 67
Louis Lussier: 27, 40, 41, 63, 80, 81
Trevor Mills: 37, 65, 113
Thomas Moore: endpapers, 15, 17, 23,
  31, 35, 39, 45, 47, 52, 53, 55, 57, 59,
  75, 77 (*detail*), 79, 87, 93, 95, 97, 99,
  100, 101, 104, 105, 111, 115
Larry Ostrom: 21, 61
Richard Siemans: 88, 89
Fiona Spalding-Smith: 71, 73, 77, 90,
  91, 102, 103, 116, 117
Henk Visser: 33
Ken Webb: 109

Installations
Christopher Casler: 11
Micheline Lévesque: 128
© Peter Mauss/ESTO: 8, 9, 124 (*top*)
Thomas Moore: 121, 126
Fiona Spalding-Smith: 118, 120, 122,
  124 (*bottom*), 125
Feature Four Limited: 123

Artists' Photos
Russell Bingham: 88
Catherine Carmichael: 60
Paul Chapnick: 16, 18, 20, 24, 36, 40,
  42, 48, 50, 56, 58, 76, 82, 84, 86, 90,
  94, 96, 110
John Dean: 106
Louis Lussier: 26
Tawny Maclachlan: 30
Ken McGinnis: 108
Trevor Mills: 64, 112
Thomas Moore: 14, 22, 44, 52, 70, 78,
  102, 114
Abbey Newman: 54
Jeff Nolte: 38
Jacques Payette: 80
Jurgen Vogt: 12
Toronto Sun, Canada Wide,
  S. Behal: 32

Cineplex Odeon, The First Ten Years
was originally published by Cineplex
Odeon Corporation, 1989.

Design
Scott Thornley, Cara-Lynn Rumack,
Thornley/Interchange Inc.

Art Production
Charlene Codner,
Thornley/Interchange Inc.

Typesetting
Cooper & Beatty.

Printed in Canada by
Arthurs-Jones Lithographing Ltd.